LAW, SOCIETY, and POPULATION:

Issues in a New Field

LAW, SOCIETY, and POPULATION:

Issues in a New Field

Larry D. Barnett

and

Emily F. Reed

foreword by
Charles B. Nam

Cap and Gown Press
Houston

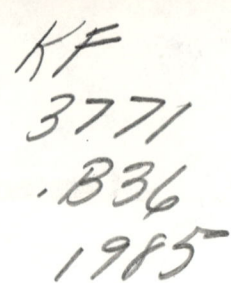

Copyright © 1985 by Cap and Gown Press, Inc.

All rights reserved.
No part of this book may be reproduced or transmitted in any form whatsoever
or by any means, electronic or mechanical, including photocopying,
recording, or by any information storage and/or retrieval system,
without written permission from the Publisher.

Cap and Gown Press, Inc.
Box 58825
Houston, Texas 77258
U.S.A.

Library of Congress Catalog Card Number: 84-71502

ISBN 0-88105-053-9 (Clothbound edition)

Printed in the United States of America

Contents

Tables and Figure	viii
Foreword	ix
Preface	xiii
Chapter I. Introduction	**1**
Brief Note on Structure of American Judicial System	6
Chapter II. Fertility	**9**
1. Sex Roles	9
2. Cohabitation and Contraception	14
3. Marriage	21
4. Pregnancy	27
5. Abortion	31
6. Illegitimacy	47
7. Child Care Facilities	49
8. Conclusion	52
Chapter III. Mortality	**67**
1. Court Decisions: Children	71
2. Court Decisions: Adults	73
3. Religious Beliefs and Affiliation	76
4. A Final Distinction	81
5. Conclusion	81
Chapter IV. Migration and Population Distribution	**88**
1. Migration Across State Lines	92
2. Local Government Control of Population Numbers	100
3. Local Government and Population Composition	110
4. School Desegregation	114
5. Government Preferences for Residents	131
6. State Preferences for U.S. Citizens	139
7. Conclusion	145
Chapter V. State Versus Federal Authority	**159**
1. State Legislatures and Political Representation	161
2. Traditional State Functions and Federal Authority	162
Chapter VI. A Look Ahead	**172**
Index	181

LIST OF TABLES AND FIGURE

Number and Title of Table:	Page No.:
2-1: Changing American Attitudes toward Cohabitation	20
2-2: Changing American Attitudes toward Premarital Sex	21
2-3: Proportion Never Married (United States)	22
2-4: Approval Rates of Legalized Abortion According to Religion, Sex, Education, Income, Race and Age, 1969-1983	37
3-1: The Individual's Right-to-Die (U.S.)	75
3-2: Public Attitudes toward Active Euthanasia (United States)	77
3-3: Relationship between Age and Disapproval of Death Options	78
4-1: Distribution of Americans 25-64 Years of Age According to Whether They Moved to a Different Home between 1975 and 1980 and the Destination of Moves	88
4-2: Preference for Place of Residence (United States)	89
4-3: Public Support in the U.S. for Government Relocation of the Urban Poor	94
4-4: Percentages Favoring and Opposing Most Efforts to Change and Strengthen Women's Status in American Society Today	99
4-5: Public Approval of Federal Equal Employment Legislation during the Post-War Period in the United States	117
4-6: Public Support for Desegregation of Travel in the Post-War Period in the United States	118
4-7: Public Acceptance of the *Brown* Decision (U.S.)	120
4-8: Part I. Support of Levels of School Integration Among White Parents of School-Age Children (United States)	122
4-8: Part II. Support of Levels of School Integration Among White Parents of School-Age Children (Southern U.S.)	123
4-9: Support and Opposition to Busing (United States)	126
4-10: Public Attitudes toward Immigration in the U.S.	142
4-11: Percentages Favoring and Opposing Legislation Making Employment of Illegal Aliens Unlawful in the U.S.	144
5-1: Public Attitudes toward Government in the U.S.	161
5-2: Public Attitudes toward Mandatory Retirement in the U.S.	165
5-3: Support for Strengthened State Governments in the Early 1980s in the United States	166
Figure 1. Trend in Approval and Disapproval of First Trimester Abortion, 1969-1983	34

Foreword

Like most emerging scholarly fields, the study of law and population has been developing very slowly and students of the subject have been experiencing difficulty in defining its scope and content. We can say, however, that "population law" is coming to mean the body of knowledge that encompasses the various paths through which legal norms and practices have a bearing on population structures and processes and, in turn, the ways in which those structures and processes have served to create and modify legal structures and activities.

While one may discover some writings relevant to this area of concern far back in history, it is clear that serious attention to the topic itself is of very recent vintage. Much credit must go to Luke Lee and his colleagues at The Fletcher School of Law and Diplomacy who set up a Law and Population Programme in the early 1970s that generated a series of books and monographs on issues pertaining to the field of population law. A perusal of recent books and journals in the areas of law and of social science reveals a growing interest in the subject matter.

No single publication as yet exists which is comprehensive in its coverage of this new field. It is no wonder, since the categories of law and population that would have to be traversed are numerous and their interrelationships often complex. On the population side, one must be concerned with population growth and decline; the basic components of population change, namely, fertility, mortality, and geographic mobility; population composition; demographic and social characteristics; and population distribution. A host of subtopics suggest themselves, including various means of fertility control, health and morbidity, immigration, urbanization, and age, sex, and racial-ethnic distributions. On the legal side, one must consider legislative forms such as constitutions, treaties, statutes, executive orders, administrative regulations, and ordinances, and jurisdictional forms reflected in a number of court systems, all of which can appear at international, national, or local levels.

Both the law itself and those positions associated with it (legislators, judges, magistrates, executive officers, commissioners, and their staffs) constitute a large bundle of legal elements that can impinge upon population conditions. The normal, incremental process of accumulating wisdom about these matters will lead us, ultimately, to some encyclopedic volumes that cover the full range of issues.

In recent years, there have been few attempts to draw together the segments of knowledge in this area. However, a great deal of attention has been given to some parts of the taxonomy outlined above and virtually no attention has been given to other parts. In particular, there has been much written about fertility control (especially abortion, sterilization, and other contraceptive practices) and about organized efforts by governments and private agencies to intercede with policy formulations.

Law, Society, and Population: Issues in a New Field takes a more eclectic approach than most former excursions into this area by broadening the population agenda to cover most aspects of the population classification suggested. It is somewhat restrictive on the legal side by limiting coverage to court decision, but legislative and sociological linkages are frequently introduced. The content provides the authors with a great enough task in an area still relatively uncharted. The rest of the legal elements in conjunction with the range of demographic categories can well make up another volume.

The authors come to their subject with outstanding credentials. Larry Barnett had the unique preparation of doctoral study in sociology, with emphasis on family and population, and training in the law. He has taught both the social sciences and law, has been affiliated with organizations in both areas, and has conducted research on both demographic and legal topics. He studied population and law in the Netherlands under a Fulbright Scholarship, and he established and now edits a prominent journal entitled *Population Research and Policy Review*. Emily Reed, who received a doctorate in political science, has background in public opinion and policy aspects of law and also brings to the book a second perspective on the subject.

In the next couple of decades, the new field of population law may well develop into a broad discipline with a flourishing professional structure and an extensive agenda, and scholars will look back at this volume as a stepping stone in its development. Right now, it represents one of the most thorough treatments of a field that has become more and more vital for understanding the population dynamics of our time and its consequences.

Charles B. Nam

Florida State University

Preface

This volume presents a perspective on court cases that has not, to my knowledge, been systematically explored. We will argue that court cases dealing with the constitutionality of government action do not occur at random, that both the occurrence of and the decision in such cases reflect societal structure and the forces affecting it, and that the cases can be understood only within their social context. In support of this thesis, empirical research from social science — particularly from sociology — is extensively used in order to suggest the factors account for the cases examined. Since this research did not explicitly consider court action, the volume can only be suggestive, but my hope is that the book will help persons working in the field of law to appreciate the potential utility of sociology in their endeavors and that it will also motivate sociologists to examine court decisions in their research. Sociology has matured as an empirically-based discipline to a point where close collaboration between it and law can be profitable to both.

This book is the result of diverse influences over a period of many years. It could not be otherwise, for in proposing the thesis that societal attributes are instrumental in the occurrence and outcome of court decisions, the book explores a completely ignored intersection of two fields — sociology and law — that have largely gone their separate ways. Although I am undoubtedly not aware of all of the influences that led me to the intersection and the thesis, the intellectual seeds for the journey seem to have been planted by two individuals.

While a student at the University of Florida law school (1973-1975), I had the opportunity to attend a colloquim given by the late Justice Tom C. Clark of the U.S. Supreme Court. During the session Justice Clark remarked that, because of the limited enforcement powers of the judiciary, he would not vote to accept a case for review unless he was convinced that the American people were ready for and would accept the decision the Court was likely to render. The colloquim, which provided an unusual insight into the processes leading to Supreme Court decisions, helped to sensitize me to the social context of judicial action.

The second person playing a role in the development of the thesis of this book is also someone I encountered as a student at the University of Florida law school — Professor Scott Van Alstyne. Although I never had him for a class, Scott stressed in one of the many conversations we had that an essential aspect of good law teaching is continual concern with the social policies that courts are attempting to advance in their decisions. In the years I have spent in law teaching, I have never forgotten his point, and attention to the social objectives motivating courts led me to an increasing appreciation of the tie that exists between court action and society.

Both of the preceding experiences occurred after I was trained in sociology, and that training undoubtedly contributed to the impact that each had. The training, however, was critical for an additional reason: It familiarized me with the type of empirical research available in sociology. The process of locating and incorporating the research bearing on the social context of the court decisions examined in this book was fascinating. The advances that have been made in macro-sociology in the past ten years are truly impressive, and this work would not have been possible without them.

In the preparation of the manuscript, it was my good fortune to have had the assistance of Emily Reed. Our backgrounds are complementary — mine in sociology and law, hers in political science — and as a result she took responsibility for the public opinion data that were needed while my efforts focused on legal and sociological materials. Dr. Reed also helped in developing and refining ideas for the project. While one can explore uncharted territory alone, it is more effective to do so with a companion.

Larry D. Barnett

January 1984

Reprint Acknowledgements

The authors wish to thank the copyright holders for permission to reprinted quoted materials. Materials from *Public Opinion* are reproduced with the permission of the American Enterprise Institute.

Chapter I.
Introduction

There appears to be a growing awareness of the existence of complex, pervasive interrelationships between legal and population phenomena. The study of these interrelationships is only in its infancy, but it offers impressive potential. Law both affects demographic processes and reflects them. Unfortunately, the number of scholars actively pursuing this study is small — in the United States, no more than a half-dozen at this writing — but a broader base of interest seems evident. Indeed, the Population Association of America has recognized the study as a distinct specialty.[1]

This book was undertaken in order to develop further the interrelationships between legal and population phenomena, but given the considerable breadth of the field and the variety of topics that fall within its purview, this work necessarily focuses on only one type of interrelationship. Specifically, the concern of this volume is with court decisions relevant to demographic processes and the social forces from which those decisions emanate. Because of inadequate data, the link is not subject to precise quantitative assessment at this time, but we are convinced that the link exists, and the book will suggest directions for research on it.

Law is a diverse discipline, and the emphasis here is with only one of its facets — court decisions. For most persons, including professional demographers, statutes enacted by legislatures and regulations adopted by administrative bodies constitute the most familiar facet of law, but statutes and regulations on their face are often difficult to apply to specific situations or are perceived as inequitable. Court challenges to their application and constitutional validity thus frequently arise, and the resulting adjudication reveals social conditions and trends at work within law. Court challenges necessarily involve disputes between parties each of which possess reasonable, but conflicting, viewpoints. Particularly in cases found in appellate courts, "there are few areas of the law in black and white. The greys are dominant and even among them the shades are innumerable. For the eternal problem of the law is one of making accomodations between conflicting interests."[2] In dealing with challenges to statutes and regulations, those accomodations derive from a societal context. One aspect of that context is the values and attitudes of the public regarding the issues involved.[3]

The law is normally a reactive institution, following rather than leading developments elsewhere, and this is particularly true of courts, which can act only when disputes are brought to them for resolution. This is not to say that courts cannot and do not influence subsequent events; they surely do, at times affecting demographic processes through impacts on the very fabric of social organization.[4] But courts do not initiate lawsuits, and the types of disputes that are taken to courts stem from conditions and changes in society. It is no accident, for example, that laws banning abortion were taken to and considered by the U.S. Supreme Court in the early 1970s rather than the early 1950s. Moreover, the decisions rendered by judges reflect the nature of society; it is thus not by chance that the Court held restrictive abortion laws to be unconstitutional in the early 1970s.

Court decisions offer an especially fertile source for scholarship, in part because they are accompanied by statements identifying and explaining legal considerations that support them. Those statements, commonly referred to as *court opinions*, are useful not just as guides for determining future decisions in factually-similar settings. They are also a means to identify the social forces influencing the perceptions and decisions of the judiciary. Court opinions are thus a useful source of data for studying the interrelationships between law and its societal context.[5]

Court decisions involving statutes and regulations — and their supporting opinions — will be the focus of this book, but such court decisions are of different types. They may deal with the application of statutes and regulations to specific situations that are not clearly covered by their expressed terms, or they may deal with the validity of statutes and regulations under the U.S. Constitution. In the latter case, the issue is whether the statute or regulation is consistent with the basic legal document of the American Nation. The issue is the same for both federal and state governments. The federal government can act only when the Constitution provides it with the authority to do so and its action does not violate any limitation that source imposes. A state government derives its authority from its own constitution and an evidently inherent police power to protect the health, safety, morals, and welfare of its citizens, but the federal Constitution imposes restrictions on a State that cannot be violated.[6]

Because the determination of the constitutionality of government action is both a difficult and a weighty process, this book is largely devoted to it. Constitutional adjudication is difficult because the provisions of the document with which we will deal are general statements of public purposes and ideals that must be applied to specific, concrete problems. It is weighty because the judiciary is standing in the shoes of those who placed the provisions in the document and is interpreting them according to the goals that motivated their adoption.[7] In the Constitution, Americans

> undertook to carry out for the indefinite future and in all the vicissitudes of the changing affairs of men, those fundamental purposes which the instrument itself discloses. Hence we read its words, not as we read legislative codes which are subject to continuous revision with the changing course of events, but as the revelation of the great purposes which were intended to be achieved by the Constitution as a continuing instrument of government.[8]

Constitutional provisions are the result of difficult problems confronting society in the past, and their interpretation requires that the basic objectives and policies they represent be carried forward into the future and applied to new types of problems. Because of the competing values involved in those problems and the general nature of constitutional provisions — whose interpretation necessarily provides relatively few guidelines — constitutional adjudication is particularly useful for revealing the fundamental philosophies of the country and their link to public attitudes.[9]

It should perhaps be underscored that the restrictions which are imposed by the Constitution (for example, as to sex discrimination) and with which we will deal in this book are applicable to government and not to private parties. Thus persons in the private sector may treat males and females differently in situations in which goverment cannot make such a distinction. Statutes and regulations may proscribe conduct for private parties if the proscriptions are consistent with constitutional provisions, but here it is legislation, not the Constitution, that is regulating behavior. Private parties will not be subject to constitutional restrictions unless government has provided significant encouragement to and is responsible for their conduct or unless they are exercising functions that traditionally have been the exclusive prerogative of government.[10] However, situations in which private parties are held to have acted on behalf of government are comparatively few in number; indeed, private organizations receiving all of their funds from government are considered to be private in nature and not subject to constitutional strictures without additional types of government involvement in their operations.[11]

Because they will be repeatedly encountered in this book, two restrictions that the Constitution imposes on federal and state (including local) governments should be introduced now. The first is the **due process guarantee**: Government cannot deprive a person of "life, liberty, or property without due process of law." The second is the **guarantee of equal protection**, which restricts the ability of government to classify persons and to treat the classes created differently. Governmental action that restricts the liberty of individuals, limits the use they make of their property, or treats them differently because of some difference in attributes is not necessarily invalid.

Three tests exist to determine whether governmental action is acceptable under these guarantees (which emanate from the Fifth and Fourteenth Amendments). In the least stringent test, a statute or regulation is constitutional if it can be reasonably thought to advance a legitimate public interest. In the intermediate test, a statute or regulation is constitutionally valid if it substantially furthers an important public interest. In the most stringent test — imposed when there is a serious impact on a fundamental constitutional right or when there is a class that is constitutionally suspect because of severe legal, political or economic disabilities — government action is valid only if it advances a compelling public interest by the narrowest possible means. As one proceeds from the least to the most stringent test, then governmental action can be constitutional only as its goal is increasingly important to the welfare of society and its precision in promoting that goal improves.

The situation in which one test rather than another is used and the way in which each test is applied will be found in the chapters to follow, but clearly the choice of the appropriate test determines the likelihood that the government will prevail. The choice also provides evidence of the certainty of the judiciary that it has identified "'principles sufficiently absolute to give them roots throughout the community and continuity over significant periods of time, and to lift them above the level of the pragmatic political judgments of a particular time and place.'"[12] The more severe the test, the greater the certainty in this regard.

Court challenges to statutes and regulations have not occurred at random but have developed around two types of issues involving the distribution of political power in the United States. In the first and most frequent type of issue, individuals have claimed exemption from government prescriptions and proscriptions. Here, the individual has been pitted against government, and whether the government is federal, state or local has been irrelevant. In the second type of issue, courts have had to resolve disputes between state govenments and the federal government over which had authority to act in a situation. Individual rights *vis-a-vis* government were not in contention, as in the first type of issue; rather, the question was which government can regulate the conduct of individuals.

The two types of issues can develop in the context of each of the three basic demographic processes — fertility, mortality, and migration. Given the frequency of litigation over the first issue, a chapter is devoted to government regulation of the individual for each demographic process. Chapter II thus deals with government - individual conflict over matters related to fertility; Chapter III concerns such conflict with regard to mortality; and Chapter IV focuses on that conflict as it has arisen within the context of migration and population distribution. The second type of issue, however, has been the subject of only limited litigation, and as a result, Chapter V covers state government - federal government conflict with regard to all of these demographic processes.

In concluding this introduction, the importance of knowledge concerning the link between societal conditions and constitutional law should be noted. Both the legal profession and the social sciences stand to benefit from that knowledge. To the extent the societal conditions are identifiable that facilitate or impede a court decision in favor of a party challenging the constitutionality of government action, lawyers can more easily determine whether to encourage or discourage a client wishing to mount or defend such a challenge. Given the considerable investment of time, money, and emotion in litigation — as well as the importance of avoiding unfavorable court decisions and their influence as precedents in future litigation — it is important to maximize the predictive accuracy of legal advice. Social scientists, for their part, will have an improved grasp of the workings of society and its legal institution. Their ability to predict the emergence of and decision in socially significant court cases increases the utility of their craft. For the legal and social science communities, then, the subject of this book holds the promise of important benefits. However, before those benefits can accrue for population-related issues, social scientists concerned with demographic problems must become familiar with constitutional law and lawyers must come to appreciate research in social science. The materials in the chapters to follow is an initial step toward accomplishing this.

A Brief Note on the Structure of the American Judicial System

In the United States, both the federal government and each of the states have judicial systems, and the systems are structurally similar in many respects. Each has trial courts, intermediate appellate courts, and a court of final jurisdiction, usually named the supreme court. In the federal system — on which this book will primarily focus — the trial courts are labelled district courts and are organized along state lines; each state is the home of at least one federal district court, and more populous states have several. Appeals from district court decisions are normally taken to the Courts of Appeals, which are organized geographically into entities called circuits. There are twelve circuits to handle cases from the district courts, with each circuit (other than that for the District of Columbia only) including at least three states. Appeals from decisions of a Court of Appeals may be taken to the U.S. Supreme Court — as may a limited range of decisions from federal district courts and state appellate courts — if that Court agrees to accept the cases. While the Courts of Appeals are required to review cases taken to them, the Supreme Court is not.[13]

Both the federal and state judicial systems may assess the

validity of statutes and regulations under the U.S. Constitution. State statutes and regulations can be tested constitutionally in either state or federal courts, but federal statutes and regulations can be tested only in the federal courts.

NOTES

1. Population Association of America (1981). *1980 Directory of Members*, Washington, D.C.

2. Estin v. Estin, 334 U.S. 541, 545 (1948).

3. Joel B. Grossman and Austin Sarat (1971). "Political culture and judicial research," *Washington University Law Quarterly* 1971: 177-207. Benjamin I. Page and Rovert Y. Shapiro (1983). "Effects of public opinion on policy," *American Political Science Review* 77: 175-190.

4. Ronald R. Rindfuss, John S. Reed, and Craig St. John (1978). "A fertility reaction to a historical event: Southern white birthrates and the 1954 desegregation ruling," *Science* 201: 178-180.

5. Charles A. Thrall (1983). "Legal images of the family in the United States: An exercise in using law as data," *Population Research and Policy Review* 2: 53-65.

6. The validity of the statutes and regulations of a State may be assessed under the constitution of that State and under the Constitution of the United States. It is only the validity of statutes and regulations under the U.S. Constitution that will concern us, since our focus is on the nation as a whole.

7. *See generally* McCulloch v. Maryland, 17 U.S. (4 Wheat.) 316 (1819).

8. United States v. Classic, 313 U.S. 229, 316 (1941).

9. The United States Supreme Court has expressly acknowledged the role of public attitudes and values in a number of decisions involving constitutional issues relevant to social demography, *e.g.*, Roe v. Wade, 410 U.S. 113 (1973) (abortion); Santosky v. Kramer, 455 U.S. 745 (1982) (termination of rights of parents to their children).

10. Blum v. Yaretsky, 457 U.S. 991 (1982).

11. *Id.;* Rendell-Baker v. Kohn, 457 U.S. 830 (1982).

12. Plyler v. Doe, 457 U.S. 202, 218 n. 16 (1982), quoting from page 114 of Archibald Cox (1976). *The Role of the Supreme Court in American Government*. New York: Oxford University Press.

13. For a thorough description of the federal judicial system, see Charles A. Wright (1983). *The Law of Federal Courts*. 4th ed. St. Paul, Minnesota: West.

Chapter II.
Fertility

This chapter deals with fertility within the context of governmental regulation of the individual. Specifically, our concern here is with situations in which some level of government — federal, state or local — attempts to regulate various aspects of human sexuality and reproduction, leading to judicial decisions regarding the constitutionality of such regulation. The cases in this chapter are organized according to the sequence of events that individuals can experience in entering the status of parenthood. Cases will be presented on the basis of the successive stages through which young adults may pass as they become, or avoid becoming, parents.

We will begin with the extent to which government can influence the formation and content of sex roles, since the degree of divergence or similarity between the roles of men and women influences the level of fertility.[1] From there we will consider in turn the ability of government to deter cohabitation of unmarried persons, to restrict access to marriage, to refuse to provide financial benefits during pregnancy, and to limit the availability of abortion. Proceeding through this sequence takes us to the point of parenthood, and assuming a pregnancy has been carried to term, we will deal with illegitimacy and child care facilities. The constitutional ability of government to act in these areas, and thus impose or alleviate the burdens of children, can be expected to affect the probability of childbearing.[2]

1. Sex Roles

We turn our attention first to cases involving sex segregation in public educational institutions. As we shall see, such segregation may have the purpose of enhancing educational efficacy by recognizing the existence of role differences, or it may have the purpose of promoting the different roles that have traditionally existed for males and females in American society. Court opinions to date indicate that the former purpose is constitutionally justifiable but that the latter purpose is not. In *Vorchheimer v. School District of Philadelphia,* [3] a challenge was mounted to the maintenance of separate academically-oriented, college-preparatory high schools for the two sexes. Other high schools in the same system offered courses needed for college admission and were coeducational, but the two segregated "academic" high schools were characterized by a reputation for scholastic excellence. The plaintiff in the case was a female who preferred to attend the academic high school for males, but she was unable to provide evidence that the school for females would cause her any injury. The two academic high schools were found to be generally equal in quality and course offerings, with the plaintiff thus expressing only a personal preference for the school for males. Under these circumstances, the U.S. Court of Appeals for the Third Circuit (which covers the states of Pennsylvania, Delaware, and New Jersey) held that the sex segregation at issue did not violate the guarantee of equal protection provided by the Constitution [4]— a guarantee that limits the ability of government to classify individuals.[5] The view of the court was that equality of educational opportunity existed between the two academic high schools and that, since females could attend coeducational high schools offering courses for college admission, attendance at a sex-segregated academic high school was voluntary. Accordingly, constitutional requirements were believed satisfied. In reaching this conclusion, the court acknowledged the existence of different sex roles for males and females and expressed its approval of sex segregation in the public schools where the purpose was to promote the educational process:

> Equal educational opportunities should be available to both sexes in any intellectual field. However, the special emotional problems of the adolescent years are matters of human experience and have led some educational experts to opt for one-sex high schools.[6]

The personal problems facing young adults, noted by the court, are in some measure the result of courtship and mate selection, a process that implicates the societally-defined differences between the sexes.[7] Research evidence suggests that schools that are limited to members of one sex may be educationally advantageous by eliminating from the classroom student concern with sexual pairing and mate selection.[8] The research even permits the argument that single-sex schools may have the effect of reducing disparities in traditional sex roles by permitting individuals to concentrate on personal advancement rather than adherence to role expectations — "to be themselves" rather than to be what is socially expected of them.[9]

However, sex segregation may have the purpose of promoting social and economic differences between males and females, and it is in this area that constitutional barriers loom large. For example, in *Mississippi University for Women v. Hogan*,[10] the U.S. Supreme Court held that a State was constitutionally impotent to operate an all-female nursing school even though it also had coeducational nursing schools on campuses located in other areas. However, the Court was careful to limit its holding to the facts of the case before it, expressly noting that it was not faced with the situation as in *Vorchheimer* where sex segregation existed between schools in the same geographic area that were equivalent in quality and curriculum.[11] The Court suggested that single-sex schools will be approved if they both serve "important governmental objectives" and are "substantially related" to the advancement of those objectives. With regard to the first part of this test, a governmental objective is not acceptable if it is based on "fixed notions concerning the roles and abilities of males and females;" with regard to the second part,

> the purpose of requiring that close relationship [between an important objective and the segregation] is to assure that the validity of a classification is determined through reasoned analysis rather than through the mechanical application of traditional, often inaccurate, assumptions about the proper roles of men and women.[12]

The statistical dominance of women in nursing led the Court to the conclusion that the all-female nursing school at issue had the purpose of continuing the societal definition of nursing as an occupation appropriate only for women. However, the Court did not address the ability of government to operate sex-segregated schools in order to preserve different personal attributes considered desirable by society for the two sexes. Indeed, the Supreme Court in other decisions has emphasized economic issues when invalidating governmental action that discriminated on the basis of sex roles.[13]

An underlying theme is apparent in the *Vorchheimer* and *Hogan* decisions that emanates from the distinction between occupational and personal attributes. When government has the purpose of promoting the educational process by segregating males and females because of the interference with education caused by gender differences in personal attributes, even though those differences are societally derived, the action is constitutionally valid. However, the segregation is invalid when its purpose is to reinforce traditional differences in the occupational roles that the two sexes have pursued. At least with regard to occupational attributes, men and women are constitutionally entitled to equality of opportunity and training. Their personal attributes may differ — e.g., the greater emphasis on noncompetitiveness and altruism for females[14] — but not their economic possibilities.

Sociological research suggests that those personal attributes are important in determining the occupational careers of men and women. By mid-life, the two sexes receive roughly equivalent benefits from the number of years of education they undertake, though this is evidently not because of continuous returns to women on their educational investment but because that investment provides the credentials utilized by women to re-enter the labor force after interruptions due to family responsibilities. At the same time, women generally do not increase their occupational status during their working lives. Among the reasons for this are the interruption of their careers in order to meet family responsiblities and the commitment to certain types of occupations (particularly those permitting ready re-entry). Thus, a recent study concludes,

> Given the complex allocation process [for occupational status] that we have observed, the strategies for producing equality of opportunity for men and women are not obvious. Extending the chances for advancement of women in female-dominated occupations would clearly improve the situation. Also, women should have increased opportunities to obtain the graduate and professional education necessary for entry into the higher professions and higher

levels of administration in both the private and public sectors. But this is not enough. We think it unlikely that much progress will be made in reducing occupational (or economic) inequalities between the sexes unless and until sex role socialization differences and occupational sex typing are substantially reduced.[15]

Constitutional imperatives can remove formal, government-imposed barriers faced by members of one sex in gaining entry to occupations, but the informal barriers stemming from the sex-role definitions prevailing in American society — the societally-assigned personal traits and occupational identifications emphasized by the study above — seem largely beyond the reach of the law. Constitutional guarantees against sex discrimination began to be the serious concern of the U.S. Supreme Court after American attitudes toward sex roles began changing at an escalated rate. Egalitarianism appears to have been increasing since the early 1950s, but the rate of change evidently underwent a noticeable rise in the first half of the 1970s.[16] It was at this point in time that the Supreme Court undertook to provide Americans with substantial constitutional protections against gender-based discrimination by government.[17]

It is questionable, however, whether further attitudinal change on the part of the public in the future will create similar advances. Constitutional philosophy seems to have gone about as far as it will go,[18] and future cases can be expected simply to deal with additional situations (probably not large in number) under that philosophy.

It is thus significant that there is evidence of a major reduction currently underway in the identification of occupations with one sex or the other, signalling a trend toward minimizing social views regarding the "proper" jobs for women and men.[19] If this trend fully develops, it will be the societal assignment of different types of personal attributes — personality traits, if you will — to women and men that constitutes the one remaining basis for differentiation in the world of work. In view of the evidence suggesting that gender differentials in earnings do not stem from invidious employer discrimination,[20] sex distinctions appear to be now a social rather than a constitutional problem.

In conclusion, it is useful to suggest directions that research should pursue in order to identify the causal factors in sex-role change. In this regard, it is important that research focus on *societal* rather than *individual* characteristics — on the components of the social structure rather than on the elements defining the individual — for it is change in the societal fabric that induces change in institutions such as law. In the context of sex roles, research needs to identify the attributes of society that have been instrumental in promoting an egalitarian ideology over the past several decades. Unfortunately, there is little empirical basis for the development of testable hypotheses, but it is probable that increasing affluence, knowledge, and population density have been important. Let us take each of these three variables in turn, although they have probably acted in concert:

As affluence rises, there is an enhanced opportunity for activities in which individuals can explore their own interests and experiment with different lifestyles. Affluence provides the time and resources needed to consider alternatives to existing modes of behavior.[21] Further, the rapid growth in knowledge has fueled specialization along intellectual lines.[22] With a distinction developing in terms of field of knowledge, distinctions on the basis of other criteria — gender included — have necessarily become less important. The human mind seems capable of responding to only a limited number of features in its social and physical environment, and as a new feature competes for attention, others are inevitably less influential. But knowledge does more than simply supply a competing basis for social distinctions. It probably reduces the importance of stereotypes, including those grounded on gender, by providing a criterion for social classification that emphasizes ability and performance.[23] Finally, increased population density and the concomitant growth in interpersonal contacts have increased the number and types of stimuli impinging on individuals, promoting their opportunity to develop along other lines than those dictated by traditional sources.[24]

2. Cohabitation And Contraception

We turn now to the subject of the cohabitation of members of the opposite sex who are not married to one another, a phenomenon that has undergone a dramatic increase since 1970, when it was negligible in frequency. The number of unmarried **couples** in the United States who were cohabitating and with whom no children were living jumped from 29,000 in 1970 to 305,000 in 1980 where the householder (the person in whose name the home was owned or rented) was less than 25 years of age. Where the householder was aged 25 through 44 years, there was an equally impressive change — from 60,000 couples in 1970 to 537,000 in 1980.[25] Among these two groups, there has been roughly a tenfold increase in cohabitation. Although the causes of the rapidly increasing incidence of cohabitation are not clear, it is believed that the appearance in the last two decades of highly effective contraceptives — particularly the pill and IUD — was a major factor.[26] We thus will begin our discussion with an examination of the constitutional rights of American citizens to have access to contraceptives.

The U.S. Supreme Court has clearly expressed its view that government cannot prohibit or even seriously restrict the availability of medically nonhazardous contraception except in highly-circumscribed situations. In *Carey v. Population Services International*, decided in 1977, the Court considered and invalidated a statute that limited the distribution of nonprescription contraceptives to licensed pharmacists only.[27] The Court concluded that governmental restrictions, even if the restrictions do not completely prohibit their sale and distribution, are unconstitutional unless the restrictions are necessary to advance a compelling governmental interest and are the narrowest means possible for advancing that interest.

> [T]he same test must be applied to state regulations that burden an individual's right to decide to prevent conception or terminate pregnancy by substantially limiting access to the means of effectuating that decision as is applied to state statutes that prohibit the decision entirely. Both types of regulation may be justified only by a compelling state interest and must be narrowly drawn to express only the legitimate state interests at stake.[28]

In the case before it, a limitation on the distribution of nonprescriptive contraceptives to pharmacists and hence to a small proportion of potential outlets was seen by the Court as a significant interference with the rights of the individual under the Constitution, and since there were no compelling governmental interests involved, the limitation was invalidated. Indeed, there are probably few limitations on the availability to adults of medically-safe contraceptives that could survive a constitutional challenge.[29]

In the decade prior to the *Carey* decision, the availability and use of contraceptives had become increasingly prevalent in American society. In 1965 an estimated two-thirds of married women in their childbearing years used some kind of contraception. A decade later an estimated three-fourths did so.[30] The influence on cohabitation of the acceptability and availability of contraception is suggested by a small 1972 survey of college couples who had cohabited for at least three months.[31] The study. which found these living arrangements to be highly satisfying to their participants, concluded that the ready availability of contraceptives was an enabling condition for the relationships. Significantly, most of the cohabiting couples viewed their relationships as alternatives rather than preludes to traditional marriage, believing that cohabitation provided freedom and equality to women as partners rather than confinement and subjugation that they considered to exist in traditional marriage. However, even if cohabitation is viewed as a preliminary to marriage — a conclusion suggested by a study of a nonrandom sample of university students who expected to have children but who were generally reluctant to do so while unmarried[32] — the availability of contraceptives is essential for cohabitants, and the prevalent use, moral approval, and social importance of contraceptives — both for the public in general and the highly individualistic segment preferring cohabitation to marriage — indicates that the Court's decision in *Carey* reflected overwhelming public support.

What is the source of the constitutional right of Americans to have ready access to medically-safe contraceptives? The question is important, for its answer helps us to understand further ramifications of the right. The Supreme Court has pinpointed the source in the protection of liberty found in the due process guarantee of the Constitution, which provides that government cannot deny "any person of life, liberty, or property without due process of law."[33]. The protection of liberty has been held to create a constitutional **right of privacy** that excludes government from seriously interfering with personal decisions in the area of marriage and family life except in the presence of compelling circumstances. Thus the restriction on the ability of government to place restrictions on contraceptives exists "not because there is an independent fundamental 'right of access to contraceptives,' but because such access is essential to exercise of the constitutionally protected right of decision in matters of childbearing."[34] The availability of contraceptives is part of a package of rights available to Americans under their constitutional guarantee of personal autonomy with regard to marriage and family matters.

Should the right of privacy protect those who are unmarried? The Supreme Court has emphatically stated that marriage is the cornerstone of society,[35] and such a philosophy would argue for discouraging sexual relationships outside the matrimonial bond. The constitutional umbrella, in this view, would not seem to provide protection to those who damage the essence of our social fabric. Nonetheless, the Court has concluded that, insofar as access to contraceptives is concerned, the right of privacy includes the unmarried. Although the Court has not explicitly done so, the extension of the right to the unmarried can be based on the fact that, by its very wording, the due process guarantee applies to "any person" and is not conditioned on the presence of certain types of attributes. It is the human individual who is to be protected rather than a relationship. The Supreme Court expressed itself in 1972 as follows:

> [T]he marital couple is not an independent entity with a mind and heart of its own, but an association of two individuals each with a separate intellectual and emotional makeup. If the right of privacy means anything, it is the right of the *individual*, married or single, to be free from unwarranted governmental intrusion into matters so fundamentally affecting a person as the decision whether to bear or beget a child.[36]

The principle that the American legal system should maximize the autonomy of the individual from governmental restrictions appears not only within the constitutional realm but outside as well; it is a policy that can be found in several areas of law. Indeed, constitutional adjudication is very much based on social philosophies that court decisions in seemingly diverse legal fields follow. The judiciary responds to and reflects social forces in a generalized manner and applies the principles derived from the American cultural heritage in the varied disputes coming before it for resolution.[37] Of course, as the result of the diversity and change that are hallmarks of the United States, those philosophies are not and do not remain uniform throughout the country, and thus courts in different regions may reach inconsistent conclusions when faced with similar factual situations. An examination of the philosophies behind judicial action is thus essential to an understanding and integration of judicial decisionmaking and trends.

An excellent illustration involving the use of public policy, the recognition of the impact of social change, and the application of the principle of maximizing individual autonomy is found with regard to cohabitation in the field of contract law. In the well-known case of *Marvin v. Marvin*,[38] the Supreme Court of California held that unmarried persons who had lived together may, upon separating, require their former partners to divide assets with them that were acquired during the course of that relationship. The division can be based on an express (oral or written) contract, a contract inferred from the conduct of the partners during their relationship, or a "quasi-contract" resulting not from the intentions of the partners but the need to avoid injustice. A contract emanating from cohabitation was judicially-enforceable in California, said the court, as long as it did not inseparably stem from an agreement by one partner to pay for the sexual services of the other. Nonmarital cohabitation grounded in the exchange of sexual access for economic or other benefits (such as social status) — i.e., a meretricious relationship — would violate public policy and would preclude a legally-enforceable contract, but public policy was not damaged by recognizing such contracts when cohabitation did not have this feature. Indeed, the court believed that failure to enforce such contracts could provide an incentive to avoid marriage by asset-producing partners who wanted to maximize their ability to retain their earnings. The enforceability of such contracts was viewed as at least neutralizing the motivation of some cohabiting individuals to avoid marriage and furthered the public interest in fostering the marital relationship. Among California couples who cohabit for the purpose of companionship and mutual assistance, then,

> we believe that the prevalence of nonmarital relationships in modern society and the social acceptance of them, marks this as a time when our courts should by no means apply the doctrine of the unlawfulness of the so-called meretricious relationship.... To equate the nonmarital relationship of today to such a subject matter is to do violence to an accepted and wholly different practice.... The mores of the society have indeed changed so radically in regard to cohabitation that we cannot impose a standard based on alleged moral considerations that have apparently been so widely abandoned by so many. Lest we be misunderstood, however, we take this occasion to point out that the

structure of society itself largely depends upon the institution of marriage, and nothing we have said in this opinion should be taken to derogate from that institution.[39]

The *Marvin* decision, rendered in 1976, represents a divergence from the rule traditionally enforced in the United States, and a few states have expressly rejected the decision.[40] However, a number of states have already followed it[41] as a result of changing attitudes of the public toward cohabitation and premarital sex throughout the early and middle 1970s. Let us now examine that change.

Table 2-1 suggests that attitudes during the past decade became more tolerant of living arrangements other than traditional marriage. In 1970, only two out of ten persons in the general American public believed that "trial marriages" yielded better marriages. However, by the mid-1970s, acceptance of living together was found among five or six out of every ten Americans. Indeed, three-fourths of adult women in 1980 thought that more couples will live together without marriage in the future.

At the same time, there was increasing approval of cohabitation among American youth. While only three out of ten youths in 1970 thought that living together was a good idea, by the latter part of the same decade about four out of ten high school seniors approved. However, among first-time college students during the 1970s, support for living together before marriage remained at a relatively steady level of between four and five out of ten, with some evidence of a possible decline in the last part of that decade.

Concerning the related question of premarital sex (Table 2-2), acceptance was also strong, with no evidence whatever of a decline. Approximately three in four young persons approved of premarital sex during the 1970s, when the incidence of premarital intercourse in this group rose rapidly.[42] Among the public at large, an increasing proportion accepted the phenomenon, and while roughly half in the mid-1970s viewed premarital sex as wrong, at least two in five persons (43%) did not find it so.

To summarize this section, there has been an increased public acceptance of premarital sex and of cohabitation. Given the changed attitudes of society and particularly of young people within it, along with the widespread use and high effectiveness level of contraception and the availability of abortion to deal with unintended pregnancies,[43] the pressures for marriage that traditionally existed have subsided and seem likely to continue to decline. Cohabitation of unmarried persons can thus be expected to increase in frequency, and the judiciary is likely to embrace *Marvin* in time where state legislatures have not done so by statute.

Table 2-1. Changing American Attitudes toward Cohabitation

	1970	1974	1975	1976	1977	1978	1979	1980
General Public								
Trial Marriages Yield Better Marriages		20%*						
(Don't Yield)		(73%)*						
General Public								
Cohabitation Not Morally Wrong					54%			
(Morally Wrong)					(46%)			
Adult Men								
Approve of Living Together				60%				
Adult Women								
More Will Live Together In Future								77%
High School Seniors								
Living Together a Good Idea	30%**		35%	41%	39%	40%	37%	37%
(Not Good Idea)	(61%)		(48%)	(44%)	(45%)	(43%)	(47%)	(46%)
Do Not Disapprove of Cohabitation***				71%	73%	73%	70%	69%
(Disapprove)				(22%)	(21%)	(21%)	(24%)	(25%)
First-Time College Students								
Couples Should Live Together Before Marriage			45%	47%	49%	48%	46%	44%	44%

*Estimates based on unweighted averages of percentages of men and women.
**Survey of nationwide youth.
***Responses are the totals of those who replied that "a man and woman who live together without being married are" either "experimenting with a worthwhile alternative life style" or "doing their own things and not affecting anyone else."

SOURCES: A.E. Bayer and Gerald W. McDonald (1981). "Cohabitation among youth: Correlates of support for a new American ethic," *Youth and Society* 12: 387-402.
The Harris Survey Yearbook of Public Opinion 1970 (1971). New York: Louis Harris & Associates, at 408, 465.
L.D. Johnson, J.G. Bachman, and P.M. O'Malley (1976, 1977, 1978, 1979, 1980, 1981). *Monitoring the Future, 1975, 1976, 1977, 1978, 1979, 1980*. Ann Arbor, MI.: Institute for Social Research, University of Michigan Press.
"The 70's, decade of second thoughts," *Public Opinion* 3 (December/January 1980): 19-43; p. 27.

Table 2-2. Changing American Attitudes toward Premarital Sex

	1969	1970	1972	1973	1975	1976
General Public						
Premarital Sex Not Wrong (Wrong)	21% (68%)	34% (60%)	(70%)	43% (48%)	43% (48%)	
College Students						
Premarital Sex Not Wrong (Wrong)			66%* (33%)**		79% (19%)	79% (19%)
Unimportant Person Married Be a Virgin (Important)		73% (25%)				
18-24 Year Olds						
Premarital Sex OK If In, or Not In, Love (Not OK)			76% (23%)			

* Estimates based on unweighted averages of percentages of men and women.
** Estimate based on 2 to 1 ratio of "not wrong" to "wrong" answers.

SOURCES: "American attitudes on sex, nudity have undergone dramatic changes" (1973). *Gallup Opinion Index*, Report No. 98: 22-27.
  George H. Gallup (1972). *The Gallup Poll, Public Opinion: 1959-1971*. New York: Random House.
  George H. Gallup (1978, 1979, 1981). *The Gallup Poll, Public Opinion: 1972-1977* (2 vols.), *1978, 1980*. Wilmington, DE.: Scholarly Resources.
  George H. Gallup (1972). "Is there really a sexual revolution?" *Gallup Opinion Index*, Report No. 85: 23-29.
  The Harris Survey Yearbook of Public Opinion 1970 (1971). New York: Louis Harris & Associates, at 465.

3. Marriage

The rising incidence of and changing attitudes toward cohabitation and premarital sex are indications of an increased resistance to marriage on the part of young Americans. Nevertheless, it is still true that the vast majority marry. The proportion of Americans never married rose noticeably between 1970 and 1980 among both men and women, yet even in the latter year six out of seven women and three out of four men had tied the proverbial marital knot before their thirtieth birthday.[44]

Table 2-3. Proportion Never Married (United States)

Age	Women 1980	Women 1970	Men 1980	Men 1970
25 years	28%	14%	43%	27%
29 years	15%	8%	24%	14%

Surveys of public attitudes toward marriage indicate that marriage is generally accepted and approved as the predominant living arrangement in today's society. For example, three-fourths of women surveyed in 1975 and 1980 believed a married life with children to be the most personally satisfying life style for them.[45] Similarly, a majority of students aged 19 to 22 who were surveyed in 1969 and in 1977 preferred the "present form of marriage" to any other living arrangement. However, the proportion of these students with a preference for the current form of marriage declined from 69 per cent in 1969 to 57 per cent in 1977.[46] Among adults generally, the proportion holding negative opinions toward never marrying declined from about half in 1957 to one-third in 1976. Additionally, the proportion of adults who believed marriage alters a person's life favorably declined about one-third during the same period.[47]

Curiously, in spite of this evidence of some disillusionment with marriage, there was a substantial increase between 1969 and 1977 in the proportion of college students expecting to marry. While 51 per cent expected in 1969 to have the present form of marriage, 70 per cent had the same expectation in 1977.[48] Data for high school students are comparable for the period commencing in the mid-1970s: The proportion of high school students who thought that they would eventually choose marriage held steady at about three-fourths btween 1975 and 1980.[49] The apparent contradiction in the decline in preference over time for marriage as a lifestyle, and the increase over time in personal expectations for living in the present form of marriage, seems to indicate a realistic reconciliation of idealism and practicality. Although fewer young people would prefer the current form of marriage, more realize that it is likely to be their own living arrangement, that is, that they will be unable personally to abandon the traditional, predominant lifestyle.

Although an overwhelming majority in national surveys in the U.S. in the 1970s rated a happy family life as the most important personal value, this percentage appears to have declined slightly (from 80 per cent in 1973 to 74 per cent in 1978),[50] and seven out of ten in 1978 no longer fully believed that married people are happier than unmarried people.[51] Americans tend to rate traditional marriage and family life as a persistent ideal, but they are also realistice enough to expect that the reality of marriage and family life often will not meet that ideal.

In view of the importance assigned to the marital relationship and the increased recognition of its deficiences, it is curious that there has been little research on the specific factors inducing marriage among Americans. It does appear that definite social pressures foster marriage within a certain age-range[52] and that events and experiences disrupting the life cycle (e.g., military service) are the only ones that can seriously affect marriage age in American society.[53] Accordingly, while there has been and will probably continue to be acceptance of alternative living arrangements, the marital institution will almost certainly remain prevalent, making constitutional protections given the individual for access to marriage of both current and future significance.

The courts have reflected the societal commitment to marriage in interpreting the Constitution. They have thus erected barriers to severe governmental restrictions on the ability to marry, but also recognized that social needs justify some controls. The leading Supreme Court decision on the right of the individual to enter marriage is *Zablocki v. Redhail*, decided in 1978.[54] At issue was a state statute requiring that individuals who were under court order to support a minor child not in their custody secure court permission to marry. That permission was not to be granted until it was demonstrated that the applicant was in compliance with the support order and that the child(ren) covered by the order were not currently welfare recipients and were unlikely to become such. The plaintiff challenged the constitutionality of the statute when, because he was the father of an out-of-wedlock child receiving welfare benefits and had not made any payments pursuant to a court order to support the child, he was not able to obtain a license to marry a(nother) woman with whom he was expecting a child.

In stating its view that marriage is essential to individual and social well-being, the Court explicitly found that marriage decisions are protected by the right of privacy that stems from the due process guarantee of personal liberty. Access to marriage is thus within the constellation of rights emanating from the constitutional guarantee of personal autonomy in the area of sexuality and procreation. In spite of the dangers to marital stability associated with out-of-wedlock pregnancies and births[55] — dangers that might have led to the conclusion that government should have the ability to impede access to marriage among those having engaged in conduct associated with marital dissolution — the Court rejected the position that marriage under such conditions should fall outside the severe restrictions placed on governmental regulation by the right of privacy.

> It is not surprising that the decision to marry has been placed on the same level of importance as decisions relating to procreation, childbirth, child rearing, and family relationships.... [I]t would make little sense to recognize a right of privacy with respect to other matters of family life and not with respect to the decision to enter the relationship that is the foundation of the family in our society.[56]

Because the statute at issue seriously restricted access to marriage and infringed the right of privacy, it could be constitutional only if based on a compelling public interest and employed the narrowest possible means to attain that interest. However, the Court found that the interests asserted by the State — that the statute provided an opportunity to counsel applicants regarding their existing obligations and that it provided an incentive to make support payments and prevent children from becoming public dependents — were insufficient, unnecessary, or nonexistent. A marriage license could not constitutionally be denied after counseling was completed, and any incentive to support children either was available through other means or was illusory. The restriction was illusory in that it did not prevent persons subject to it from undertaking financial obligations apart from marriage that would reduce the likelihood they would be able to make support payments, and it prevented applicants from undertaking marriages that would improve their financial position and enhance their ability to make the payments. Accordingly, the statute was found to impose an unwarranted restriction on access to marriage upon one class of persons and to violate the constitutional guarantee of equal protection.

Given the heavy burden imposed on government by the compelling interest standard and the usual invalidation of government action subject to this standard, it is clear that the entire matrix of regulations governing marriage cannot be evaluated by the test, and the Court expressly acknowledged this. Regulations that do not seriously abridge the right of privacy will be tested by whether they reasonably appear to further a legitimate governmental purpose. The questions to be examined, then, are the situations in which the right of privacy protects marriage and the kinds of regulations which seriously interfere with the right. The right of privacy presumably does not protect all facets of marriage, and not all regulations seriously abridge the right even when it is implicated. Under either of these conditions, governmental action is evaluated only in terms of whether it is reasonably related to a legitimate public interest.

Only court decisionmaking over time will determine when these conditions exist, but a recent case is illustrative. In controversy was a state statute that required individuals under 18 years of age to obtain parental consent if they wished to marry, even if the female was prematurely pregnant. [57] In deciding against the use of the compelling interest test, the court distinguished *Zablocki* on the grounds that the regulation of minors was not involved there. The constitutional authority of government to protect minors from their inexperience and vulnerability and to promote parental control led the court to conclude that the statute should be tested by the standard of reasonableness. The access of minors to marriage was not viewed as implicating the right of privacy; while minors are not devoid of constitutional rights, those rights do not have the same reach as they do for adults.[58] Since there was a legitimate public interest in avoiding the unstable marriages to which minors are particularly prone[59] and since this interest could be deemed reasonably likely to be advanced by requiring parental consent for minors who wished to marry, the statute was held to be constitutionally valid.

If the right of privacy is not involved when government places restrictions on the access of minors to marriage, it is involved but not seriously infringed when government uses marriage as an indicator of dependency to deny eligibility for welfare benefits[60] or as an indicator of a possible conflict of interest to deny employment to persons who are married to one another and who are (or would be) working together.[61] The right of privacy, moreover, is implicated but not seriously affected when a husband and wife are required to pay more in income taxes than they would if they were not married and simply lived together.[62] Government action that merely provides an incentive or disincentive for marriage is not a serious intrusion on the right of privacy and thus is tested by whether it is reasonably related to a legitimate public purpose. Only those actions of government that determine the conditions under which marriage may take place have the potential to constitute serious infringements on the right of privacy: "A classification based on marital status is fundamentally different from a classification which determines who may lawfully enter into the marriage relationship."[63]

In conclusion for this section, let us discuss briefly the characteristics of society that may have fostered change in the acceptability of cohabitation and marriage over the preceding decades. The discussion will hopefully stimulate research, for if future trends are to be predicted, those characteristics and the nature of their influence must be identified.

There are two societal conditions that appear to deserve attention in the context of cohabitation and marriage: affluence, and the range and change of stimuli in the environment. To the extent that affluence allows the critical minimum needed by individuals for self-support, there is the possibility of escaping dependence upon others. When continuation of a relationship is not economically necessary, the probability that living partners will alter is enhanced.[64] The greater affluence now available to women thus appears to be an important factor in the higher incidence of divorce.[65]

At the same time, the heterogeneity of and rate of transformation in the stimuli to which members of society are exposed undoubtedly influences patterns of behavior. To the extent that stimuli in the environment are diverse and changing — as the result of such factors as high population density and technological advances — there will be a greater opportunity for new commitments in general and a greater inclination toward impermanent interpersonal relationships in particular.[66] Tolerance of extramarital sexuality is thus greater in large cities than elsewhere.[67] In environments in which there is a variety of and variation in stimuli, high rates can be expected in cohabitation and, to the extent marriages occur, marital dissolution. These rates are both reflected in and facilitated by the extent of legal protections provided nonmarital relationships and marital access.

4. Pregnancy

While voluntary childlessness can be expected to increase substantially in the United States,[68] pregnancy will probably still be experienced by a majority of women. The view of pregnancy taken by the courts is thus important. Since large numbers of married women will almost certainly continue to work outside the home in order to maintain the family's desired lifestyle,[69] we will examine the legal protections that exist from constitutional adjudication and statutory enactments to protect female employees who are pregnant and want to continue working before and after childbirth. Recent information is not available on the proportion of married women who work during pregnancy, but in the early 1970s four out of ten did so.[70] Following delivery, many return to the labor force; in 1978, three out of ten married women 18 to 34 years old who had a child less than one year of age were employed.[71] These rates represent an apparent departure from traditional patterns and are likely to increase further.[72]

The U.S. Supreme Court dealt in the 1970s with a number of cases involving the denial of employment-related benefits during pregnancy, and these cases constitute the most significant body of court opinions that are concerned with the issue of pregnancy outside of contraception and abortion. The first case involved a state-operated mandatory disability insurance program for persons in private employment.[73] The program, which was funded solely by employee contributions, excluded normal (but not abnormal) pregnancy and childbirth from the disabilities covered. The exclusion was challenged on the ground that, since only women become pregnant, the program discriminated on the basis of gender, but the Court held that there was no violation of the guarantee of equal protection. There was no evidence of an intent to discriminate against women; rather, the program was seen as intended to be a viable insurance scheme and to classify not persons but disabilities. The classification was upheld because it was reasonably related to the state's constitutionally-legitimate goals of maintaining the self-supporting nature of the program and minimizing the premium, which most burdened those with the lowest earnings.

Even though the program covered conditions afflicting only males while excluding normal pregnancy, the Court refused to find discrimination on the basis of gender. Critical to its position was its view of the state's purpose behind the establishment and operation of the program. Not only was there an absence of evidence of an intent to engage in sex-based discrimination — the lower premiums resulting from the pregnancy exclusion, for instance, were enjoyed by women as well as men — but there was evidence that women received benefits that exceeded their contributions and, hence, more benefits than men. The Court summarized its position as follows:

> Absent a showing that distinctions involving pregnancy are mere pretexts designed to effect an invidious discrimination against the members of one sex or the other, lawmakers are constitutionally free to include or exclude pregnancy from the coverage of legislation such as this on any reasonable basis, just as with respect to any other physical condition.[74]

Sex discrimination will not be found where benefits to males and females are equal, but will be where one sex suffers greater burdens than the other. Disability insurance that excludes pregnancy while otherwise providing equivalent benefits to both sexes precludes a finding of sex disrcimination, but the policy of an employer that requires females on maternity leave to forfeit accumulated seniority constitutes impermissable sex discrimination by imposing "on women a substantial burden than men need not suffer . . . because of their differing roles in the scheme of human existence."[75]

Two other cases illustrate an alternative approach in assessing the constitutionality of governmental action concerning pregnancy. At issue in the first case were the policies of two public school systems requiring pregnant teachers to take unpaid leave at least four months before their expected delivery.[76] The policies clearly had the purpose of regulating the conduct of persons on the basis of pregnancy, and thus the Court concluded that they seriously affected the right of privacy. In holding the policies invalid, the Court found that the governmental interests involved — continuity of instruction and elimination of physically-incapacitated teachers from the classroom — were important but could be achieved with less of an infringement on the right. Continuity of instruction was attainable by permitting the teacher to select the date for beginning her leave but requiring her to provide ample advance notice, and the elimination of teachers incapacitated by their pregnancies was possible through mandatory examinations by a physician. At the same time, there was an unnecessary constitutional infringement in the policy of one school board that precluded a teacher from returning to work until the first semester after her child reached three months of age. While a teacher may be prevented from re-entering the classroom until a new semester has begun, the requirement that the child reach three months of age was unacceptable because of its inflexible nature. Individualized determinations were constitutionally required in gauging readiness to return to work just as they were required in determining inability to continue to work. For the same reason, a statute was invalidated in a second case because it classified women as ineligible for unemployment compensation during the twelve weeks before childbirth and the six weeks after. "The Fourteenth Amendment requires that unemployment compensation boards no less than school boards must achieve legitimate state ends through more individualized means when basic human liberties are at stake."[77]

Constitutional philosophy thus accepts incidental effects on pregnant women when government acts with the intent of promoting other legitimate goals, but pregnant women cannot be the object of governmental action merely *because* they are women or *because* they are pregnant. Pregnancy is a socially-valued condition that is protected by the Constitution from intentional, invidious treatment. This view, however, reflects an ideal that is not fully shared by the American public. Many employers are fearful of the inconvenience and economic cost of pregnant employees,[78] and there is evidence that pregnant women are discouraged from participating in situations involving contact with others,[79] which presumably includes the work setting. This attitude, though, seems likely to subside. As sexuality loses its negative aura and comes to be publicly accepted, so probably will pregnancy Moreover, the view of pregnancy under the Constitution may be an ideal that deviates from prevailing attitudes — a deviation whose extent unfortunately cannot be determined with existing evidence — but it is an ideal whose divergence from reality is probably not great.

By way of conclusion for this section, it is useful to suggest the societal factors affecting the salience of pregnancy as a legal issue. The Supreme Court cases examined here were decided in the mid-1970s, but the factors that generated them were necessarily operating in prior years. One factor that may have been influential is the occupational structure of the national economy. It appears that the rate of growth in high status jobs fell just before the Court decisions after being at a higher, stable level for some two decades.[80] The relatively rapid change during these two decades may have generated a sensitivity to traditional restrictions and disabilities imposed on employees, including those associated with pregnancy, for social change can be expected to result in questions regarding established practices in general. Perhaps more importantly, the decline in the rate of expansion in desirable positions — with its negative consequences for upward mobility — increased the importance of eliminating burdens on employed women and the impetus to do so. If the long-term advance in equalitarian sex-role attitudes was to be incorporated into a labor market having fewer attractive positions than had been expected, society had to free women from restraints on participation in that market.

A second factor may have been at work to increase the constitutional visibility of pregnancy. Research suggests that the probability of pregnancy is directly affected by the number of housing structures per unit area; as housing density rises, the incidence of pregnancy falls.[81] Housing density evidently increased markedly in the early 1970s; the average annual increase in the number of households was 1.8 per cent during the 1960s but 2.5 per cent in the 1970-1973 period — a jump of 39 per cent.[82] The pressures that increased housing density placed on the inclination of couples wanting to create a pregnancy logically would have induced attempts to eliminate other burdens on pregnancy. Society's interest in childbearing will be manifested in the actual, or at least attempted, elimination of constraints to pregnancy that are removable without serious economic or social disorganization, as are those challenged in the Supreme Court cases above.

5. Abortion

Abortion has become a prevalent phenomenon in the United States in a short span of time. It has been estimated that, as of 1981, approximately 18 per cent of all women 18 to 44 years of age had had a legal abortion since state legislatures began to liberalize statutes regulating the procedure in the late 1960s.[83] In a single year, abortions now are performed on roughly three per cent of all women of reproductive age and terminate approximately 30 per cent of all pregancies. These levels, while evidently having largely stabilized, have increased markedly since the U.S. Supreme Court invalidated restrictive abortion laws in 1973.[84]

The 1973 decision of the Court, *Roe v. Wade*,[85] is undoubtedly one of the landmark cases of the twentieth century. In the controversy it has generated, it ranks with the holding in *Brown v. Board of Education*[86] that racially segregated schools resulting from intentional governmental action are unconstitutional. Indeed, the 1980 platform of the Republican Party called for a constitutional amendment to prohibit abortion and several bills to that end have been considered in Congress.

The legal aspects of the decision in *Roe v. Wade* are relatively straightforward. Faced with a state statute that imposed criminal penalties for all abortions except those needed to save the life of the pregnant woman, the Supreme Court found a serious interference with the right of privacy that emanates from the liberty guarantee of due process:

> The detriment that the State would impose upon the pregnant woman by denying this choice altogether [to terminate her pregnancy] is apparent. Specific and direct harm medically diagnosable even in early pregnancy may be involved. Maternity, or additional offspring, may force upon the woman a distressful life and future. Psychological harm may be imminent. Mental and physical health may be taxed by child care. There is also distress, for all concerned, associated with the unwanted child, and there is the problem of bringing a child into a family already unable, psychologically and otherwise, to care for it. In other cases, . . . the additional difficulties and continuing stigma of unwed motherhood may be involved.[87]

Given the impact of laws that seriously restrict access to abortion, the Court applied its most stringent test of constitutionality, requiring that the governmental action advance a compelling interest by the narrowest possible means. Under this test, the Court noted, the right of privacy was not absolute but subject to regulation under highly circumscribed conditions. In the context of abortion, government could act to protect its compelling interests in the health of the woman and the potential life of the fetus.[88] Those interests reach importance at different points in the gestation process, and as they do, increasing governmental restrictions become justified on the freedom of the woman to decide on a course of action regarding her pregnancy. After the risk of death from abortion equals or exceeds the risk of death from childbirth — roughly commencing with the second trimester of pregnancy[89] — government possesses a compelling interest in regulating the abortion procedure in order to protect the health of the pregnant woman, and reasonable regulations to this end — e.g., in terms of the type of facility in which the procedure is performed[90] — are permissible. After the fetus becomes viable — roughly at the start of the third trimester — government can ban abortion unless the procedure is necessary to protect the life or health of the pregnant woman.

> The decision leaves the State free to place increasing restrictions on abortion as the period of pregnancy lengthens, so long as those restrictions are tailored to the recognized state interests. The decision vindicates the right of the physician to administer medical treatment according to his professional judgment up to the points where important state interests provide compelling justifications for intervention. Up to those points, the abortion decision is inherently, and primarily, a medical decision, and basic responsibility for it must rest with the physician.[91]

In its opinion, the Court expressly acknowledged that societal problems played a role in its deliberations. Even though the focus of the right of privacy is on individuals and their intimate relationships, the Court admitted that the contours of the right are influenced by the issues which its members perceive to be important to national life. "This holding, we feel, is consistent with . . . the demands of the profound problems of the present day," problems which included "population growth, pollution, [and] poverty."[92] The permissible boundaries for personal autonomy, as defined by the Supreme Court, are thus to some extent influenced by the public's perception of large-scale issues. In its allusion to population growth, for instance, the Court was reflecting public concern over this issue. Data indicate that public concern over population growth and overpopulation was highest in the years prior to the *Roe* decision.[93]

An historical look at attitudes toward abortion and how these attitudes have changed over time further elucidates the manner in which court decisions interact with public opinion on major societal problems. The question of legalized abortion did not become an important social and political issue until the mid-1060s. Consequently, data on abortion attitudes prior to that time are scarce. However, in the early 1960s the relationship of the drug thalidomide to birth defects prompted some pregnant American women who had used thalidomide to seek abortions in European countries where abortion was legal. A 1962 opinion poll indicated that more than half (52%) of the American public approved of such actions.[94]

In 1965, public opinion on the legalization of abortion in a variety of situations apparently began to coalesce, and thus national surveys started to measure it. In that year, 11 per cent of American adults thought that abortion should be legalized for pregnancies that create a serious danger to the woman's health, carry a strong chance of a serious defect in the baby, result from rape, involve an unmarried woman, cause economic hardship in a low-income family, or involve a married woman who wants no more children. In 1972, 36 per cent shared that view, and after the *Roe* decision in 1973, roughly four out of ten thought abortion should be legal, a level that has remained generally stable.[95] Thus, "the largest part of the change in abortion attitudes occurred before 1970, simultaneously with campaigns to liberalize state abortion laws. While [*Roe* appears] to have boosted levels of approval further, the sharpest changes had by then already taken place."[96]

The interrelationship of the *Roe* decision with public opinion is further clarified by an examination of the public's approval and disapproval of legalized first-trimester abortion without regard to circumstances — that is, abortion on demand — for the 1969-1983 period. *Roe* precluded governmental interference with first-trimester abortions, and attitudes toward such abortions have been tapped by national surveys much more frequently than attitudes toward the reasons justifying abortion in general, permitting a more precise analysis of the link between public opinion and *Roe*. Figure 1 illustrates the trend in public opinion.

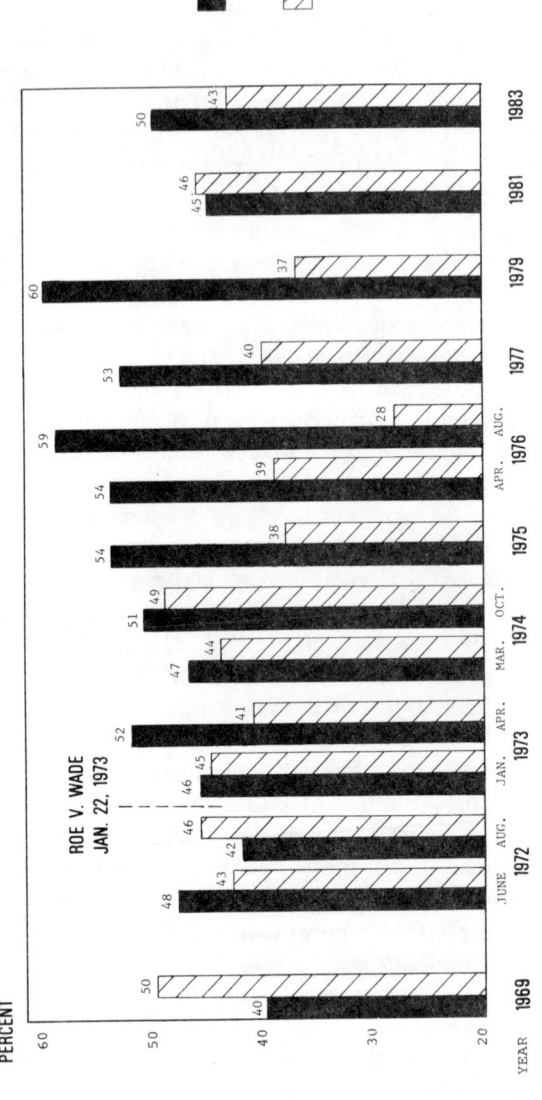

FIGURE I. TREND IN APPROVAL AND DISAPPROVAL OF FIRST TRIMESTER ABORTION, 1969-1983

SOURCES: E.M. Uslaner and R.E. Weber (1980). "Public support for pro-choice abortion policies in the nation and states; changes and stability after the *Roe* and *Doe* decisions," in C.E. Schneider and M.A. Vinoskis (eds.), *The Law and Politics of Abortion.* Lexington, MA.: D.C. Heath, Table 1, p. 209.
The Harris Survey Yearbook of Public Opinion, 1970. New York: Louis Harris & Associates, at 465.
"Public rejects income surtax, would cut defense budget and impose wage/price regulations" (1974). *Gallup Opinion Index,* Report No. 113: 1-17.
George H. Gallup (1978). *The Gallup Poll, Public Opinion, 1972-1977.* V. 1. Wilmington, DE.: Scholarly Resources, at 94, 247.
"Public evenly divided on issue of abortion during early stage of pregnancy" (1981). *The Gallup Report,* Report No. 190: 18-22.
"Public remains closely divided on Supreme Court's 1973 abortion ruling" (1983). *The Gallup Report,* Report No. 215: 16-18.

Between 1969 and 1972, the level of approval of first-trimester abortion fluctuated within a limited range of between four and five out of ten. During this period, public opinion was split at an average of 43 per cent for and 46 per cent against legalized first-trimester abortion, with an average of 11 per cent undecided.[97] Consequently, by 1973 there was by no means support from a majority (or even a decisive plurality) for the Court's decision with regard to first-trimester abortions. In fact, in the months immediately prior to the release of the *Roe* decision, there is some evidence of a decline in approval of first-trimester abortion. Approval dropped from 48 per cent in June, 1972, to 42 per cent in August, 1972. Similarly, disapproval increased from 43 per cent in June, 1972, to 46 per cent in August, 1972. On January 28, 1973, approximately one week after the release of *Roe*, there was a slight increase (four percentage points) in public approval of abortion. Three months later in April, 1973, approval had risen to a majority (52%).

This increase in approval of legalized first-trimester abortion and the corresponding decline in disapproval can be attributed to the "rallying around the flag" effect[98] which often follows a controversial public policy decision. When such a decision has been made, the general public tends to come to the support of the high-level decisionmaker. The public reaction appears to be based on the belief that the new approach ought to be given a chance to work and that a decision by an important arm of the government is presumably correct. In the case of the *Roe* decision, the rallying effect was manifested in the 1973 polls, and the Court may have reversed what was the start of a decline in public approval.

A year after the decision, however, a slight decline in support indicates that the rallying effect had dissipated, so that the small but solid increase in support for legalized first-trimester abortion from 1975 through 1979 can be attributed both to the long-range effect that the Court's decision had in shaping public attitudes toward abortion and related issues that occurred during this period.[99] Between 1975 and 1979, public support for legalized first-trimester abortion on demand averaged 56 per cent, slightly higher than a simple majority and 13 points higher than the average for the 1969-1972 period. Approval for legalized abortion on demand peaked in 1979 at three out of five persons.

In 1981, attitudes toward legalized abortion during the first trimester slipped back into an even split between approval and disapproval. The 15-point drop in approval from 1979 to 1981 corresponds to the apparent decline of liberal attitudes toward related issues which occurred around the end of the 1970s.[*100*] This decline indicates that the effect of the *Roe* decision on public opinion had run its course and that other factors now superseded it. However, in 1983 support for abortion rebounded, with a majority again approving.[*101*]

The attitudes of the public as a whole are only a part of the abortion issue. The attitudes of various segments of society are also important, and in this regard we find differences in approval levels, differences which illustrate further dimensions of the abortion issue. Table 2-4 presents the breakdown of abortion attitudes during the 1969-1983 period for each of six demographic variables. (The change in the questions used in the table was necessary in order to follow the demographic groups throughout the period.)

Religious affiliation has generally been thought to be an important determinant of abortion attitudes. Specifically, given the strong stand of the Roman Catholic Church against abortion in all circumstances, it is commonly believed that, first, the majority of opponents of legalized abortion would be Catholics and that, second, the majority of Catholics are characterized by unfavorable attitudes toward legalized abortion. The first part of this hypothesis suggests that Catholics and the Roman Catholic Church are the single most active voice opposed to abortion, a conclusion that is supported by empirical data. A recent survey of the two most vocal and organized groups active in the debate found that Catholics comprise 70 per cent of the membership of the National Right to Life Committee, which opposes abortion, but only 4 per cent of the membership of the National Abortion Rights Action League, which supports the availability of the procedure[*102*]

However, it is the second part of the hypothesis that is important here, for constitutional philosophy responds to social conditions rather than to pressure groups. During the 1969-1983 period, as Table 2-4 indicates, the level of approval of abortion was less among Catholics than among Protestants.[*103*] Moreover, the difference between the two groups evidently increased after *Roe*: There was a drop of four percentage points in Catholics' approval level approximately a year following the decision, though the difference between the two groups lessened in subsequent years.

Table 2-4. Approval Rates of Legalized Abortion by Religion, Sex, Education, Income, Race and Age, 1969-1983 (United States)
Proportion Approving Abortion

	1969*	1973*	1974* Mar.	1974* Oct.	1975**	1978**	1979**	1980**	1981**	1983**
National	40	46	47	51	75	77	76	78	75	81
Religion:										
Protestant	40	45	48	52	76	76	79	78	75	82
Catholic	31	36	32	41	67	73	69	77	70	79
Sex:										
Male	40	49	51	54	74	77	75	75	76	81
Female	40	44	43	48	75	77	78	80	73	80
Education:										
College Grads	58	63	67	71	87	86	88	88	85	88
H.S. Grads	37	44	44	49	75	77	78	79	74	81
Grade S. Grads	31	30	25	30	55	58	52	55	54	65
Income:										
$20,000 plus	-	-	60	62	82	90	86	87	83	87
$10,000-19,999	-	-	47	58	82	77	81	75	74	81
$9,999 or less	-	-	40	41	65	65	61	68	62	68
Race:										
White	-	-	47	53	76	79	78	80	77	83
Non-white	-	-	45	40	60	55	59	65	65	69
Age:										
Under 30	46	55	55	64	81	80	79	80	80	82
30-49	39	48	44	48	77	81	81	81	77	84
50 or older	38	39	43	43	68	71	71	73	68	77

*Approval of first-trimester abortion on demand.
**Approval of abortion in some or all circumstances.

SOURCES: "Public attitudes are split over court abortion ruling" (1974). *Gallup Opinion Index*, Report No. 106: 22-24.
"Public rejects income surtax, would cut defense budget and impose wage/price regulations" (1974). *Gallup Opinion Index*, Report No. 113: 1-17.
"Stage of pregnancy is key to public approval of abortion" (1975). *Gallup Opinion Index*, Report No. 121: 11-13.
"Public backs female rights, would split over abortion law" (1976). *Gallup Opinion Index*, Report No. 128: 16-20.
"Huge majority would grant right to abortion" (1978). *Gallup Opinion Index*, Report No. 153: 25-29.
"Attitudes toward abortion have changed little since '75" (1979). *Gallup Opinion Index*, Report No. 166: 20-28.
"Attitudes toward abortion have changed little since mid-1970's" (1980). *Gallup Opinion Index*, Report No. 178: 6-7.
"Public evenly divided on 1973 decision" (1981). *Gallup Report*, Report No. 190: 18-22.
"Public remains closely divided on Supreme Court's 1973 abortion ruling" (1983). *Gallup Report*, Report No. 215: 16-18.
E.M. Uslaner and R.E. Weber (1980). "Public support for pro-choice abortion policies in the nation and states: Changes and stability after the *Roe* and *Doe* decisions," in C.E. Schneider and M.A. Vinoskis (eds.), *The Law and Politics of Abortion*. Lexington, MA.: D.C. Heath. See Table 3.

It seems likely that the greater resistance to abortion among Catholics than among Protestants delayed the emergence of the constitutional philosophy found in *Roe*.

The data in Table 2-4 thus indicate that public support for the legalization of abortion comes more from Protestants than from Catholics. In addition, men and women are not characterized by clear and consistent differences, suggesting that changes in sex-role ideology may not be causally linked to attitudes regarding abortion and the occurrence of *Roe*. However, support derives more from better-educated and wealthier persons than from those of lower socioeconomic status. These and other data [*104*] suggest that the Supreme Court tended to reflect the views of the most influential segment of American society.

Involvement of Others

Whether government can require the involvement of a person other than the pregnant woman and the attending physician prior to the performance of an abortion is an issue that has attracted measurable attention. Some controversy has revolved around the communications that can be legally required by the attending physician to the patient in order to create informed consent to an abortion. In this regard, the Supreme Court in 1983 held that a physician cannot be forced to make emotionally-laden statements — e.g., describing the fetus as an unborn human life and enumerating specified serious complications that might follow the abortion procedure —that are likely to discourage a patient from terminating her pregnancy.[*105*]

However, the involvement of others has been an issue primarily with regard to husbands when the woman is married and particularly with regard to parents when the woman is an unmarried minor. We will examine spousal and parental involvement separately, since they involve substantially different considerations. In the course of that examination, we will treat two distinct types of involvement — consent and notification. The issue in consent is whether the express agreement of the husband or parents can be a prerequisite to the performance of the abortion. The issue in notification is whether consultation of the woman with her husband or parents can be required even though she need not obtain their consent.

In 1976, the Supreme Court dealt with the issue of whether the consent of the husband could be a prerequisite to an abortion during the first trimester of pregnancy.[106] The Court has not dealt with the issue of the husband's consent in the second and third trimesters, but the issue is much less important since nine out of ten abortions are performed in the first three months of pregnancy.[107] At least in the first stage of pregnancy, however, the Court unequivocally has stated that a requirement for spousal consent is constitutionally invalid. Government cannot, said the Court, delegate to an individual veto power over an abortion sought by a woman when it does not have that power itself, and if the spouses disagree over whether a pregnancy should be terminated, the interest of the woman must take precedence inasmuch as she is the one most affected by the pregnancy. Moreover, the interest of the state in marital harmony was viewed as unlikely to be advanced by the requirement of spousal consent: "It is difficult to believe that the goal of fostering mutuality and trust in a marriage, and of strengthening the marital relationship and the marriage institution, will be achieved by giving the husband a veto power exercisable for any reason whatsoever or for no reason at all."[108]

Although data are scarce concerning public attitudes toward the issue of spousal consent, the limited information available suggests that there is a minimal public support for the judicial negation of the requirement for such consent. In 1970 only 15 per cent of married women under age 45 believed that a woman should be permitted to have an abortion in the face of the husband's opposition. In 1975, approximately one-third of both men and women approved of such abortions.[109] Further, persons who approve of legalized abortion in any circumstances would be expected to approve of abortion even in the face of spousal opposition, but only four in ten did so in 1970 and five in ten in 1977. Since persons who approve abortion in all situations are less than half of the total population, this further suggests that support for abortion without the consent of the husband is confined to a minority of Americans.[110]

The U.S. Court of Appeals for the Eleventh Circuit (which covers Alabama, Florida, and Georgia) in 1981 considered the question of whether a state can insist that the husband be provided with notice of a pending abortion.[111] The statute at issue, which expressly excluded notification where the spouses were estranged, was drafted with the intent of permitting consultation between husband and wife prior to the termination of the pregnancy. The court, finding that notification constituted an infringement of the woman's right of privacy sufficient to require a compelling public interest to be constitutional, concluded that there is a state interest of overriding importance in promoting the marital relationship and protecting a husband's concern with the ability of his wife to have children. Marriage and its concomitant, childbearing, are considered to be basic to American society and culture and are thus of compelling importance. However, as the court noted, its task involved a comparison and a balancing of two fundamental social values: The right of privacy possessed by a married woman, on the one hand, and the public interest in "ensuring that the institution of marriage maintains its authenticity," on the other.[112] The latter did not involve the quality of the interpersonal relationship but, rather, the degree to which there was congruence between the ideal form of marriage, as defined by the public through its elected representatives, and reality. Government, said the court, has a compelling interest in maximizing the congruence. This distinctly sociological approach was expressed in the following words:

> By authenticity we mean a marital relationship characterized by institutional integrity, *not* marital harmony. ...The concept we wish to convey is that the state has an interest in attempting to ensure that the institution of marriage maintains its identity with its conceptual essence. For example, the [State has] asserted that the notice provision furthers truthful and forthright communication between the spouses and mutuality of decisionmaking, which reflects Florida's notion of marriage as an ongoing, dual passage through life. The state interest underlying the regulation, therefore, is in attempting to bring the real into as close proximity as possible with the state's ideal conception.[113]

Thus defining the nature of the public interest, the court concluded that the notification requirement was less of a burden on the wife's right of privacy than it was an advantage in preserving marriage as an intact, socially-valued institution. Marriage, the court noted, is the sole state-sanctioned setting in which an individual can procreate, and procreation is a principal purpose of that institution; thus the state has a compelling interest in ensuring that one spouse does not secretly frustrate the desire of the other for a child. If notification to the husband of his wife's pending abortion advances that interest —which will be the case if abortion poses more than a minimal danger to a woman's future biological capacity to bear children — a statutory requirement to this end is constitutional.[*114*]

The court's decision appears to reflect widespread concern in the United States over high divorce rates and the apparent breakdown of marriage as a social institution. Public views on these issues are seen in several national surveys. For example, in 1970, seven out of ten men and women thought that "the institution of marriage" was weaker than it was ten years previously.[*115*] In 1978 and 1982, more than nine out of ten persons said they favor more emphasis on "traditional family ties,"[*116*] a result that is consistent with the finding that Americans usually rate a happy family life as highly important in their scheme of values.[*117*] Public concern with the stability of the institution of marriage and the family is thus pervasive, and its appearance in judicial decisions should not be unexpected.

The level of attention paid to spousal involvement pales by comparison with that devoted to the involvement of parents of a minor unmarried daughter seeking an abortion. This issue is socially significant because of the negative educational, intellectual, and psychological effects of early childbearing on teenagers and their progeny.[*118*] The issue is emotional because of the rights that parents traditionally have possessed with regard to their children and because of the proprietary attitudes of parents toward these rights. Public support appears minimal for the position that minors should have the ability to obtain an abortion without parental involvement. Thus, among those adults who approve of abortion in any circumstance — a group that is less than a majority of Americans — not even half were found in a 1977 survey to be favorable toward a minor's abortion without parental consent.[*119*]

The constitutional dictates for the issue of parental involvement are still not totally clear and fully determined, but the U.S. Supreme Court to date has dealt with the matter in several cases whose decisions suggest that constitutional law and public values may diverge. In 1976, the Court ruled that government cannot require all unmarried minors, regardless of their age and psychological maturity, to obtain the consent of their parent(s) for a first-trimester abortion.[*120*] The state interest in the authority of parents to raised their children and its interest in family unity were found to be inadequate to justify an absolute veto power by parents under all conditions, for parent-child conflict over the termination of a pregnancy would not be ameliorated by that power. Similarly, in 1979 the Court held that government cannot permit a judge to determine whether an abortion is in the best interest of the minor if one or both parents refuse to consent, for government has thereby provided a person other than the pregnant minor with absolute control over the performance of the abortion regardless of her maturity.[121] The State must make available a means to determine whether the minor is capable of understanding the nature and consequences of her decision, i.e., is mature; if she is, she may apparently undergo an abortion without the consent of, and perhaps even without notice to, her parents.[122] With regard to unemancipated minors who are not mature, however, the Court concluded in 1981 that government can insist on at least notification to the parents, where notification is possible. The bases of the decision were that such minors by definition lack the ability to make by themselves the decision that will best promote their long-term welfare and that parents in our society have a critical role in the social and psychological development of their children.[123] That role has been deemed an essential aspect of the American way of life: "Constitutional interpretation has consistently recognized that the parents' claim to authority in their own household to direct the rearing of their children is basic in the structure of our society."[124]

Public Funding

The question of whether public funds should be available to cover the costs of abortions requested by indigent women has been the source of heated political dispute and has generated litigation concerning whether there is, at least under some conditions, a constitutional requirement for such funds. In response to governmental action limiting the use of public monies for abortions sought by indigents, however, the Supreme Court has concluded that the principle of *Roe v. Wade* is not applicable and that different considerations apply. For example, in 1977 a state regulation was found constitutionally acceptable that excluded payment for an abortion desired for economic or social reasons and that allowed payment only for medically-necessary abortions [125].

In 1980 a federal statute was upheld that permitted payment for an abortion when a pregnancy jeopardized the life of the woman but not when it only threatened her health [*126*]. The latter case, *Harris v. McRae*, involved a more serious question than the former in that there was a denial of funds for a medically-necessary abortion as long as the pregnancy did not endanger the life of the woman. Since the opinion of the Court in *Harris* includes the reasoning of the earlier case and also deals with issues not covered there, let us turn to that opinion and examine it at some length.

Three constitutional issues were examined within the context of the federal statute: Whether the funding restriction unconstitutionally penalized the liberty and privacy of the individual protected by the guarantee of due process; whether it created a classification that offended the constitutional assurance of equal protection; and whether it raised certain theological beliefs to the status of a government-backed religion in disregard of the constitutional prohibition against the establishment of religion.

With regard to the first issue, the Court held that individual freedom in the area of pregnancy prevention and termination was not affected by the federal statute, because the inaccessibility of abortion to indigent women was the result of an economic situation which government had not caused. Only restrictions on abortion availability created by government itself implicate the right of individual liberty and privacy.

> [A]lthough government may not place obstacles in the path of a woman's exercise of her freedom of choice, it need not remove those not of its own creation. Indigency falls in the latter category. The financial constraints that restrict an indigent woman's ability to enjoy the full range of constitutionally protected freedom of choice are the product not of governmental restrictions on access to abortions, but rather of her indigency. Although Congress has opted to subsidize medically necessary services generally, but not certain medically necessary abortions, the fact remains that the [*federal statute*] leaves an indigent woman with at least the same range of choice in deciding whether to obtain a medically necessary abortion as she would have had if Congress had chosen to subsidize no health care costs at all. We are thus not persuaded that the [*federal statute*] impinges on the constitutionally protected freedom of choice recognized in *Wade*.[*127*]

In taking the position that it did, the Court was concerned with an important consideration having implications far beyond the abortion issue. A decision that funding for abortions was necessary would have drastically altered the character of the Constitution and the relationship of the judicial and legislative branches. It would have meant that government is constitutionally required to provide the funds needed by persons who are unable to afford items that cannot be made illegal. For instance, since access to contraceptives and private schools cannot constitutionally be prohibited, a decision in favor of abortion funding would force government to make available the funds needed by individuals who are not able to pay for them. The Constitution would thus be a source of affirmative commands, enforcible by the judiciary, that would compel legislators to enact certain types of statutes rather than being, as at present, a source of authority that permits legislators to enact statutes they desire as long as those statutes are consistent with the Nation's fundamental values.

The second issue in *Harris v. McRae* was grounded on the fact that federal funds could be used generally for medically-necessary services, including childbirth, but not for most medically-necessary abortions, leading to a classification by type of service that implicated the guarantee of equal protection. However, no impairment of the right of individual liberty and privacy existed, and indigents have not constituted a constitutionally suspect class unless their poverty has made them totally unable to pay for an item and they have thus been wholly deprived of a reasonable opportunity to obtain it [128] — a situation which, since most indigent women have been able to obtain abortions without public funds,[129] does not prevail here. Accordingly, the question is simply whether the classification by type of medical service is reasonably related to a legitimate public objective. Such an objective was found here in the preservation of potential human life. By encouraging childbirth except in a situation involving a severe threat to the health of the pregnant woman, the federal statute was reasonably related to that objective and thus, concluded the Court, did not violate the equal protection guarantee.

The third and final issue in *Harris* involved the question of whether the restriction on abortion funding incorporated religious teachings into law and thus established religion in contravention of the First Amendment.[130] The Constitution prohibits action by government that has the intent or primary effect of aiding one religious body over others or advancing religion in general, but as long as these criteria are satisfied, governmental action may be consistent with the doctrines of one or more religions. The fact that the dominant religions in the United States consider the seizure of another's property to be unacceptable behavior, for example, does not invalidate legislation punishing larceny as long as there exists a secular foundation for the law. The federal statute at issue was viewed as not constituting an establishment of religion because, while it was consistent with the views of the Roman Catholic Church, a basis for it could be found in traditional values of a moral but non-religious nature.[*131*]

Survey research indicates that the Supreme Court reflected the attitudes generally held by the public when it found acceptable the ban on public funding of abortions in most circumstances. For example, in 1970, two-thirds of American women opposed abortion at government expense. A 1975 survey indicated that 57 per cent of the general public was opposed to public funding of abortion. [*132*] A 1977 national survey taken shortly after the original Court decision upholding limitations on public payments for abortions for indigents found that a plurality (47%) favored a general ban on such payments, though almost the same number (44%) opposed it.[*133*] Thus, public opposition to the funding of abortion was declining in the several years prior to the decision, but it was still strong at the time of the decision. Moreover, the support for funding that existed seemed to lack intensity. Among persons who favor the legalization of abortion in all circumstances and who presumably would favor governmental funding of abortions, the level of support is higher than among others, but it is by no means unequivocal. In 1977, two out of three such persons approved of such funding, but only slightly more than half of them were "enthusiastic" about it.[*134*]

Conclusion

To conclude our discussion of abortion, let us consider societal attributes that may have induced the changes we have noted in attitudes toward and constitutional law on abortion. The vigorous, and often vitriolic, public debate on abortion and the conditions under which it is performed — when compared to the relative calm attending the other topics covered in this chapter — demonstrates the social depth of the issue. Curiously, however, the societal conditions are obscure that are responsible for changed attitudes toward abortion in the last half of the 1960s and the subsequent emergence of *Roe v. Wade* in the early 1970s. A clue to some of the social forces involved may be found in the fact that abortion is very much an issue linked to youth. As was previously indicated in Table 2-4, approval of first trimester abortion in the late 1960s and early 1970s was greatest among young adults; in the age-range where virtually all abortions occur — i.e., among women under 35 — the proportion of pregnancies that are terminated is noticeably higher among those under 25.[135] Abortion is thus of greatest relevance and concern to the members of the population just entering the social, economic and political world in which the citizenry functions, and it is at this entry point that society must successfully incorporate them or experience drastic cleavage and upheaval.

In this regard, it is important to note that just before and during the period when abortion attitudes were changing most rapidly — the last half of the 1960s — there was a rapid rise in the proportion that young adults constituted of the total U.S. population. Specifically, the proportion of 18-24 year olds in the U.S. population for four time-periods was as follows:[136]

1950	10.6%
1960	8.9%
1970	12.1%
1975	12.9%

The relative importance of 18-24 year olds fell during the 1950s, but the decline was sharply reversed in the 1960s, when there was a 36 per cent jump in the share that the group represented in the total population. The rise continued in the first half of the 1970s but at a slower pace. The increased prevalence and visibility of young adults in American society during the 1960s is likely to have promoted a focus on issues concerning them.

Abortion was thus an issue most salient to the age-group that needed to be incorporated into the social structure and that, in the decade prior to *Roe*, was increasing at a rapid rate numerically and becoming a more important component of society. In conjunction with these factors, there was an apparently rising level of alienation from the established political process during the 1960s that particularly affected young adults, resulting in a widening generation gap.[137] The confluence of the three factors — the age-linked nature of abortion, the changing age structure of the population, and the growing political split between new and established members of the adult citizenry — created the basis for serious age-based conflict in American society.

Viewed in this light, *Roe v. Wade* was an apparent societal response attempting to reduce age-related stress that developed in the United States during the 1960s.

> Why is it that age differences, seemingly omnipresent beneath the surface of social life, do not regularly erupt in sharp political conflicts? And when these conflicts emerge, why are the issues so often related to peace, morality, or justice?[138]

Constitutional litigation and interpretation appears to be a mechanism by which American society reduces tensions — including those occurring across age lines — that arise from issues implicating strongly-held social values. An age-stratified society requires such mechanisms, and the application of the Constitution to new social problems is logically one of them. Another, though it is generally more difficult to implement, is change in the provisions of the Constitution.[139] The Twenty-Sixth Amendment lowered to 18 the age at which the right to vote exists in all elections, and it was not chance that it was adopted in 1971. Indeed, an express goal of the Amendment was the reduction of the political alienation that had developed among young adults in the 1960s and that had been manifested in open confrontations between the younger generation and established social authority.[140] In tackling the abortion issue at the same point in history,[141] the Supreme Court was evidently acting within a larger context.

6. Illegitimacy

One of the most noteworthy trends in the last half of the twentieth century has been the rising incidence of illegitimacy. Between 1950 and 1979, the proportion of all births accounted for by unmarried women increased from 4.0 per cent to 17.1 per cent. Among whites, one out of ten births was illegitimate in 1979, but among non-whites, half were.[142] The reasons for this increase apparently include higher levels of social disorganization as well as greater cultural permissiveness that allows the negative consequences of illegitimacy to be more readily avoided.[143] Thus while a generation ago society frowned upon a woman who bore and kept an illegitimate child, in 1978 three-fourths of the public thought that "a single woman having and raising a child" was acceptable.[144]

The increased prevalence and acceptance of illegitimacy has important ramifications for society and implicates public policy, particularly since almost half of all illegitimate births are to women who are under 20 years of age[145] and births to such women have serious negative consequences of an educational and social nature for both to them and to their children.[146] The interpretation of the Constitution *vis-a-vis* the ability of government to burden and deter childbearing outside of marriage thus becomes important.

Supreme Court cases involving illegitimacy have typically arisen from governmental action that affected the children rather than the parents, and in these decisions — which commenced in 1968 — constitutional philosophy has been that government cannot punish illegitimate children, because their status is one for which they have no personal responsibility.[147] In the few cases that exist imposing penalties only on the parents, however, the apparent philosophy has been that such penalties are constitutionally valid as long as the parents have failed to pursue a reasonable opportunity to legitimate the children. Such a philosophy is consistent with public views on the morality of intentional childbearing outside of marriage.[148] Thus, in 1979 the Court upheld a statute that prohibited the father from suing for the wrongful death of a child whom he sired out of wedlock and whom he did not legitimate even though able to do so. A four-member plurality evidently received the approval of the majority-creating fifth member in stating that:

> Unlike the illegitimate child for whom the status of illegitimacy is involuntary and immutable, the appellant here was responsible for fostering an illegitimate child and for failing to change its status. It is thus neither illogical nor unjust for society to express its condemnation of irresponsible liaisons beyond the bounds of marriage by not conferring upon a biological father the statutory right to sue for the wrongful death of his illegitimate child. The justifications for judicial sensitivity to the constitutionality of differing legislative treatment of legitimate and illegitimate children are simply absent when a classification affects only the fathers of the deceased illegitimate children.[149]

Unfortunately, the number of cases involving penalties that affect only parents is negligible, making it impossible to outline definitively the types of penalties that government is capable of imposing. At the same time, the political motivation to develop such penalties may well be subsiding inasmuch as illegitimacy is apparently becoming less of an object of public disapproval. For the immediate future, then, penalties on parents to deter illegitimacy may not be forthcoming, and the development of constitutional law on the subject may be minimal.

7. Child Care Facilities

With rising rates of employment among mothers of young children, the need for financially-affordable child care has escalated and become a salient public issue. In the 30 years from 1950 to 1980, the proportion of ever-married mothers with a child under six years of age who were in the labor force more than tripled — from 14 to 47 per cent — and half of these labor force participants today are employed full-time. Accompanying this trend have been changes in child care arrangements, with increasing reliance upon nonrelatives and group care. For instance, the proportion of children under six whose mothers worked full-time and whose care was by a nonrelative or group center went from three out of ten in 1958 to five out of ten in 1977. Virtually all such child care required a financial expenditure.[150]

The attitude of nonemployed mothers with pre-school and elementary school-age children suggests that a majority of mothers do not view the lack of child care as a serious constraint on their ability to work outside the home. For example, in 1973, two-thirds of nonemployed mothers of children under age 12 thought that finding suitable child care would be no problem if they were employed. Similarly, in 1977, only one out of five mothers of children under age 5 who were not employed and not looking for work indicated that the reason for their nonemployment was a problem with the availability or affordability of child care.[151] Additionally, the high proportion of women who had pre-school children and who were in the labor force in 1980 suggests that a lack of child care was not an insuperable obstacle to employment during the 1970s among mothers of young children. Nevertheless, a growing minority of nonemployed mothers do perceive the lack of child care to be important in their nonemployment. The proportion of nonemployed women with children under age 12 who said they would certainly or probably look for work if suitable day care existed rose from three out of ten in 1970 to four out of ten in 1975.[152] Such mothers, moreover, appear to come disproportionately from young, poor, black, and poorly-educated groups,[153] suggesting that women who need employment the most have the highest probability of finding that child care is a factor in their joblessness. The unsuccessful attempt by Congress in 1971 to provide federally funded day care centers for poor women was designed to meet this need.[154]

However, the use of day care for young children so that their mothers may work, or pursue other activities, is not universally accepted. Some view child care outside the home as "an attack on the family,"[155] while others fear that it is harmful to the children, although the evidence suggests that it is not.[156] Nonetheless, a majority of the public approves of day care even when mothers of young children use it for "career purposes," "self-fulfillment," or "more leisure time," and the "money is not needed" for other purposes.[157]

Only one court decision has dealt with the question of the constitutionality of government action in the context of child care facilities. The case, which was decided by the U.S. Court of Appeals for the Ninth Circuit (which covers Alaska, Arizona, California, Hawaii, Idaho, Montana, Nevada, Oregon and Washington), involved a challenge to the alleged failure of a community college district to establish child care facilities on its own or to take advantage of opportunities to do so when the facilities could have been organized at little or no cost to the district.[158] The plaintiffs argued that the course of conduct of the defendant district disproportionately affected women and was motivated by a purpose to discriminate on the basis of gender. The court, holding that a failure to act under such circumstances can constitute a violation of the equal protection guarantee, concluded that the plaintiffs would have suffered a constitutional injury if they could prove their allegations of a disproportionate impact on women and a discriminatory purpose; the case was thus remanded for trial.

However, the court, noting the societal significance of the case, stressed the need for judicial restraint in using the Constitution as the basis for attempts to solve broad social problems. The Constitution, a source of individual rights rather than of general solution to social issues, does not permit judicial intervention into decisions of the executive and legislative branches of government except where a specific violation exists of a guarantee provided by that document.

> There can be little doubt that numerous problems of national importance lie under the surface of this litigation and that the plaintiffs have made a first move in an effort to compel the defendants to adopt a policy having pervasive implications for the community at large.... While it may be true that the plaintiffs are disadvantaged by the burdens of child rearing in their pursuit of a college education, this hardship appears comparable to a wide spectrum of conditions afflicting many other members of the student population, such as acute impediments to sight, hearing, or mobility and a narrow margin of economic self-sufficiency requiring students to be wage earners while attending college. These are problems which go to the very core of our societal organization and which affect profound social, economic, and cultural values. Surely it is not the prerogative of the judiciary to undertake the resolution of these problems, nor to review the wisdom of legislative and administrative efforts in that direction.[*159*]

In view of the explicit reluctance of the court to see the judiciary become involved in social issues on constitutional grounds — a reluctance that manifests a general principle of constitutional jurisprudence — its willingness to permit involvement with regard to child care facilities would seem to reflect the substantial public support for female employment that now exists. This leads to the question of the societal conditions responsible for the ideology favoring female employment. The answer to the question appears to lie in large part in the changing occupational structure of the country. Between 1920 and 1970, there was a steady increase in the proportion of the labor force employed in social services, but the rate of increase jumped in the decade of the 1940s and then jumped again in the 1950s and 1960s.[*160*] Given the predominance of females in social service occupations,[*161*] the rapidly expanding availability of such employment evidently enhanced the earnings potential of women and the attractiveness of labor force participation.[*162*] The greater opportunities for women in the work force were undoubtedly accompanied by an increasing incidence of careers — patterns of long-term involvement in the labor market in which there are lines of advancement (i.e., careers) and multiple career paths extending across and/or between organizations.[*163*] Careers for women necessarily require child care facilities, since it is they who have traditionally been responsible for childrearing.[164] As careers become more frequent among women in the years following World War II,[165] then concern with and support for child care facilities followed.

8. Conclusion

The material considered in this chapter suggests that federal appellate courts generally do not render decisions that affect personal autonomy relevant to fertility as a matter of constitutional law until a solid base of public (social) support exists. The base need not represent an overwhelming proportion, or even a majority, of Americans, but it evidently must be substantial. Support from roughly one-third of the public appears to be required on an issue before such a decision typically can be expected, and it is possible that the base of support in the affluent middle class is especially important.

It would be inaccurate to imply, however, that courts intentionally do not act until they are conscious that the critical level of public support exists. It is probable that cases challenging governmental restraints on individuals in areas affecting fertility are not brought and appealed until the base of public support needed for a successful challenge is at least partially present. Unfortunately, we do not know what portion of the base must exist before there will be a court challenge, what portion must exist before there will be an appeal, and what portion must exist before an appellate court having discretionary powers of review will accept a case and decide it in a given way. It may well be that, until the needed base is largely developed, potential challengers are dissuaded by the advice of lawyers, the pressure of peers, and the influence of other significant persons from taking the issue to the judiciary or at least to appellate levels. The social forces that lead to the development of constitutional law may operate at least as much by affecting the conditions under which challenges occur to governmental action as by influencing the decisionmaking process of appellate courts.

Regardless of the exact nature of the process, however, it is important to recognize that societal attributes are implicated in court determinations of the constitutionality of governmental action. As one Supreme Court justice has noted, constitutional interpretation that is durable and effective involves a "continual insistence upon respect for the teachings of history [and] solid recognition of the basic values that underlie our society,"[*166*] but the social fabric that influences the *content* of constitutional law also plays a role in determining the *time* when that law evolves.

NOTES

1. John Scanzoni (1976). "Gender roles and the process of fertility control," *Journal of Marriage and the Family* 38: 677-691.

2. *See, e.g.*, Rodolfo A. Bulatao (1981). "Values and disvalues of children in successive childbearing decisions," *Demography* 18: 1-25.

3. Vorchheimer v. School District of Philadelphia, 532 F.2d 880 (3d Cir. 1976), *affirmed without opinion by an equally-divided Court*, 430 U.S. 703 (1977). See also Williams v. McNair, 316 F.Supp. 134 (D. S.C. 1970) (three-judge court), *affirmed without opinion*, 401 U.S. 951 (1971).

4. It should be noted that, while the Supreme Court upheld the decision of the Court of Appeals, it did so without rendering an opinion. Under such circumstances, it is only the decision of the lower court that is supported and not necessarily its reasoning in reaching that decision. Zobel v. Williams, 457 U.S. 55, 64 n.13 (1982).

5. The Fourteenth Amendment expressly forbids a State to "deny to any person within its jurisdiction the equal protection of the laws." The Fifth Amendment, in preventing Congress from depriving a person "of life, liberty, or property without due process of law," has been held to provide an equal protection guarantee against action by the federal government. Hampton v. Wong, 426 U.S. 88 (1976). It is important to note that a violation of the equal protection guarantee stems from an invidious discriminatory *purpose*, not from a disproportionate impact on one group compared to another. The discriminatory purpose need not have been the sole or principal motivation for the governmental action; it is sufficient that such a purpose was present. However, the governmental action will be constitutionally valid if it would have resulted from one or more nondiscriminatory purposes that existed. Washington v. Davis, 426 U.S. 229 (1976); Arlington Heights v. Metropolitan Housing Development Corporation, 429 U.S. 252 (1977); Personnel Administrator v. Feeney, 442 U.S. 256 (1979).

6. 532 F.2d at 887. In 1983, a Pennsylvania trial court held that the sex segregation policy violated the equal protection guarantee because the two schools differed significantly in the quality of education they provided and because segregation did not benefit the psychological and social development of adolescents. Newberg v. Board of Public Education, No. 5822, Court of Common Pleas of Philadelphia County (Aug. 30, 1983). The opinion of the court appears in *The Legal Intelligencer* 189: 1, 11-15 (Sept. 9, 1983).

7. *See* Bernard I. Murstein (1989). "Mate selection in the 1970's," *Journal of Marriage and the Family* 42: 777-792.

8. Mississippi University for Women v. Hogan, 458 U.S. 718, 735 (1982) (Powell, J., dissenting).

9. Ronald Winchel, Diane Fenner, and Philip Shaver (1974). "Impact of coeducation on 'fear of success' imagery expressed by male and female high school students," *Journal of Educational Psychology* 66: 726-730.

10. Mississippi University for Women v. Hogan, 458 U.S. 718 (1982).

11. *Id.* at 720, n. 1.

12. *Id.* at 724, 725-726.

13. Weinberger v. Weisenfeld, 420 U.S. 636 (1975); Stanton v. Stanton, 421 U.S. 7 (1975).

14. Janet Lever (1978). "Sex differences in the complexity of children's play and games," *American Sociological Review* 43: 471-483. Sandra Acker (1977). "Sex differences in graduate student ambition: Do men publish while women perish?" *Sex Roles* 3: 285-299. A. Regula Herzog, Jerald G. Bachman, and Lloyd D. Johnston (1978). *Concern for Others and Its Relationship to Specific Attitudes on Race Relations, Sex Roles, Ecology, and Population Control,* Ann Arbor, MI.: Institute for Social Research, University of Michigan. Table 1.

15. William H. Sewell, Robert M. Hauser, and Wendy C. Wolf (1980). "Sex, schooling, and occupational status," *American Journal of Sociology* 86: 551-583. Quotation from p. 580; copyright 1980 by the University of Chicago. *See* Shelley Coverman (1983). "Gender, domestic labor time, and wage inequality," *American Sociological Review* 48: 623-637.

16. Otis D. Duncan (1979). "Indicators of sex typing: traditional and egalitarian, situational and ideological responses," *American Journal of Sociology* 85: 251-260. Andrew Cherlin and Pamela Walters (1981). "Trends in United States men's and women's sex-role attitudes: 1972 to 1978," *American Sociological Review* 46: 453-460. Arland Thornton and Deborah Freedman (1979). "Changes in the sex role attitudes of women, 1962-1977: Evidence from a panel study," *American Sociological Review* 44: 831-842. Otis D. Duncan (1982). "Recent cohorts lead rejection of sex typing," *Sex Roles* 8:127-133.

17. The first case was Reed v. Reed, 404 U.S. 71 (1971).

18. In *Mississippi University for Women*, the Supreme Court left open the possibility that at some point in the future it might declare gender classifications to be constitutionally suspect. 458 U.S. at 724 n.9 If gender classifications were considered suspect, their constitutionality would be determined by the "compelling interest" test rather than the "intermediate" test currently in use. Elevation of sex to suspect status appears to be the sole significant change that can be made in constitutional philosophy to reduce the ability of government to make distinctions between males and females. However, given the evidence that women can control their role in society, the likelihood does not seem great that gender will be deemed suspect, a status assigned only when there is a group requiring extraordinary protection. San Antonio Independent School District v. Rodriguez, 411 U.S. 1 (1973).

19. A. Regula Herzog and Jerald G. Bachman (1982). *Sex Role Attitudes Among High School Seniors*. Ann Arbor, MI.: Institute for Social Research, University of Michigan. *See generally* Margaret H. Marini (1978). "Sex differences in the determination of adolescent aspirations: a review of research," *Sex Roles* 4: 723-753.

20. Richard F. Kamalich and Solomon W. Polachek (1982). "Discrimination: fact or fiction? An examination using an alternative approach," *Southern Economic Journal* 49: 450-461.

21. *See* Elizabeth M. Havens (1973). "Women, work, and wedlock: a note on female marital patterns in the United States," *American Journal of Sociology* 78: 975-981. Ron Lesthaeghe (1983). "A century of demographic and cultural change in Western Europe: an exploration of underlying dimensions," *Population and Development Review* 9: 411-435.

22. For a study of the relationship between level of affluence and the rate of knowledge accumulation, see Marion Blute (1972). 'The growth of science and economic development," *American Sociological Review* 37: 455-464.

23. Evidence for this hypothesis comes by analogy from research which finds that the rigidity of the structure of organizations declines with increasing technological change. Edward Harvey (1968). "Technology and the structure of organizations," *American Sociological Review* 33: 247-259.
Between 1962 and 1977, egalitarian attitudes toward sex roles came to be correlated with educational attainment; in 1962, attitudes did not differ by educational level, but in 1977, those with more years of schooling were characterized by egalitarianism to a greater extent than those with fewer years. Arland Thornton and Deborah Freedman (1979). "Changes in the sex role attitudes of women, 1962-1977: evidence from a panel study," *American Sociological Review* 44: 831-842. However, educational level is a characteristic of the individual, while we areconcerned here with a characteristic of society, viz., its fund of knowledge. Educational attainment undoubtedly reflects to some extent, though very imperfectly, the level of knowledge possessed by society. It is important to note that in 1962, education was not related to attitudes. Even though a relationship existed in 1977, education *per se* could not have induced the trend toward egalitarianism. The relationship emerged using the same categories of educational level in 1977 as in 1962. Sex role attitude change or differential rates of change occurred *within* the various educational levels, and thus level of education could only have differentially facilitated the change. The argument here is that the growth of knowledge was the driving force in attitudinal change and in the emergence of the link between egalitarian attitudes and higher educational levels.

24. Claude S. Fischer (1975). "Toward a subcultural theory of urbanism," *American Journal of Sociology* 80: 1319-1341. *See* Bruce H. Mayhew and Roger L. Levinger (1976). "Size and the density of interaction in human aggregates," *American Journal of Sociology* 82: 86-110. *See also* Peter M. Blau, Terry C. Blum, and Joseph E. Schwartz (1982). "Heterogeneity and intermarriage," *American Sociological Review* 47: 45-62.

25. Bureau of the Census, U.S. Department of Commerce (1981). "Marital status and living arrangements: March 1980," *Current Population Reports*, Series P-20, No. 365.

26. David M. Heer and Amyra Grossbard-Shechtman (1981). "The impact of the female marriage squeeze and the contraceptive revolution on sex roles and the Women's Liberation Movement in the United States, 1960 to 1975," *Journal of Marriage and the Family* 43: 49-65.

27. Carey v. Population Services International, 431 U.S. 678 (1977).

28. *Id.* at 688.

29. The Court expressly reserved judgment on limitations reasonably concerned with the purpose of quality control, e.g., the curtailment of contraceptive distribution through vending machines. *Id.* at 691 n.11. In 1983, the Court used the First Amendment guarantee of freedom to distribute and receive information to invalidate an 1873 statute that prohibited the mailing of unsolicited commercial advertisements on contraception. The fact that some recipients of the advertisements would be offended was considered to be insufficient to suppress the flow of truthful information. In addition, the statute was found to promote only minimally the right of parents to control the education of their children regarding reproduction. Indeed, the restriction was seen as denying parents information that might be useful in deciding how to educate their children in this area. "Because the proscribed information may bear on one of the most important decisions parents have a right to make, the restriction of the free flow of truthful information constitutes a basic constitutional defect regardless of the strength of the government's interest." Bolger v. Youngs Drug Products Corporation, 103 S.Ct. 2875, 2885 (1983).

30. Charles F. Westoff and Elise F. Jones (1977). "Contraception and sterilization in the United States, 1965-1975," *Family Planning Perspectives* 9: 153-157. The high rate of usage of contraceptives by married couples in 1965 is noteworthy. In June, 1965, the Supreme Court held that a statute prohibiting the use of contraception could not constitutionally be applied to married couples. Griswold v. Connecticut, 381 U.S. 479 (1965). The decision was thus a reflection of existing societal conditions and of social forces that had already operated.

31. George Thorman (1973). "Cohabitation: a report on the married-unmarried life style," *The Futurist* 7: 250-253.

32. Ann Klimas Blanc (1984). "Nonmarital cohabitation and fertility in the United States and Western Europe," *Population Research and Policy Review* 3: 181-193.

33. The Due Process Clause of the Fifth Amendment applies to action by the federal government, and the Due Process Clause of the Fourteenth Amendment applies to the States.

34. 431 U.S. at 688.

35. Loving v. Virginia, 388 U.S. 1 (1967).

36. Eisenstadt v. Baird, 405 U.S. 438, 453 (1972).

37. For this reason, non-citizens can almost certainly be excluded from serving as judges. Ambach v. Norwick, 441 U.S. 68 (1979).

38. Marvin v. Marvin, 134 Cal. Rptr. 815, 557 P.2d 106 (1976).

39. 557 P.2d at 122.

40. Hewitt v. Hewitt, 77 Ill.2d 49, 394 N.E.2d 1204 (1979); Rehak v. Mathis, 239 Ga. 541, 238 S.E. 2d 81 (1977).

41. Homer H. Clark, Jr. (1980). *Domestic Relations*. 3rd ed. St. Paul, Minnesota: West.

42. Melvin Zelnik and John F. Kantner (1980). "Sexual activity, contraceptive use and pregnancy among metropolitan teenagers: 1971-1979," *Family Planning Perspectives* 12: 230-237. Melvin Zelnik, Young J. Kim, and John F. Kantner (1979). "Probabilities of intercourse and conception among U.S. teenage women, 1971 and 1976," *Family Planning Perspectives* 11: 177-183.

43. Rates of contraceptive utilization are found in Joy G. Dryfoos (1982). "Contraceptive use, pregnancy interventions and pregnancy outcomes among U.S. women," *Family Planning Perspectives* 14: 81-94. Data on contraceptive effectiveness are found in William R. Grady, Marilyn B. Hirsch, Nelma Keen, and Barbara Vaughan (1983). "Contraceptive failure and continuation among married women in the United States, 1970-1975," *Studies in Family Planning* 14: 9-19.

44. Bureau of the Census (1981), *op. cit.*. Data shown are from Table B.

45. Connie DeBoer (1981). "The polls: marriage - a decaying institution?" *Public Opinion Quarterly* 45: 265-275.

46. *Id.* at 267.

47. Arland Thornton and Deborah Freedman (1982). "Changing attitudes toward marriage and single life," *Family Planning Perspectives* 14: 297-303.

48. DeBoer, *supra* note 45, at 267.

49. L.D. Johnson, J.G. Bachman and P.O. O'Malley (1976-1981). *Monitoring the Future*. Ann Arbor, MI.: Institute for Social Research, University of Michigan, at 53, 92, 92, 92, 93, and 93, respectively.

50. DeBoer, *supra* note 45, at 270.

51. *Id.*

52. Linda J. Waite and Glenna D. Spitze (1981). "Young women's transition to marriage," *Demography* 18: 681-694.

53. Dennis P. Hogan (1978). "The effects of demographic factors, family background, and early job achievement on age at marriage," *Demography* 15: 161-175.

54. Zablocki v. Redhail, 434 U.S. 374 (1978).

55. James McCarthy and Jane Menken (1979). "Marriage, remarriage, marital disruption and age at first birth," *Family Planning Perspectives* 11: 21-30.

56. 434 U.S. at 386.

57. Moe v. Dinkins, 669 F.2d 67 (2d Cir. 1982), *affirming* 533 F.Supp. 623 (S.D. N.Y. 1981).

58. Ginsberg v. New York, 390 U.S. 629 (1968).

59. James A. Weed (1974). "Age at marriage as a factor in state divorce rate differentials," *Demography* 11: 361-375.

60. Zablocki v. Redhail, 434 U.S. 374, 387 n.12 (1978).

61. Keckeisen v. Independent School District, 509 F.2d 1062 (8th Cir. 1975), *cert. denied*, 423 U.S. 833 (1975).

62. Mapes v. United States, 576 F.2d 896 (Ct. Cl. 1978), *cert. denied*, 439 U.S. 1046 (1978).

63. Zablocki v. Redhail, 434 U.S. 374, 403, 404 (1978) (Stevens, J., concurring).

64. Ron Lesthaeghe (1983). "A century of demographic and cultural change in Western Europe: an exploration of underlying dimensions," *Population and Development Review* 9: 411-435.

65. Andrew Cherlin (1976). "Work life and marital dissolution," *Divorce and Separation*. New York: Basic Books.

66. Claude S. Fischer (1975). "Toward a subcultural theory of urbanism," *American Journal of Sociology* 80: 1319-1341.

67. G. Edward Stephan and Douglas R. McMullin (1982). "Tolerance of sexual conformity: city size as a situational and early learning determinant," *American Sociological Review* 47: 411-415.

68. David E. Bloom and Anne R. Pebley (1982). "Voluntary childlessness: a review of the evidence and implications," *Population Research and Policy Review* 1: 203-224; S. Philip Morgan (1982). "Parity-specific fertility intentions and uncertainty: the United States, 1970 to 1976," *Demography* 19: 315-334.

69. Valerie K. Oppenheimer (1977). "The sociology of women's economic role in the family," *American Sociological Review* 42: 387-406. The rapid increase in energy costs beginning in 1973 has placed intense pressure on the standard of living in the United States. Indeed, the purchasing power of families would have declined in the 1970s if substantial numbers of American wives had not entered the labor force. George Sternlieb and James W. Hughes (1982). "Running faster to stay in place," *American Demographics* 4(6): 17-23. It seems likely that they will be able to leave the labor force for any significant period of time in the future without jeopardizing their families' standard of living.

70. Larry L. Bumpass and James A. Sweet (1980). "Patterns of employment before and after childbirth," *Vital and Health Statistics*, Series 23, No. 4.

71. Bureau of the Census, U.S. Department of Commerce (1979). "Fertility of American women: June 1978," *Current Population Reports*, Series P-20, No. 341. Data from Table A.

72. David Shapiro and Frank L. Mott (1979). "Labor supply behavior of prospective and new mothers," *Demography* 16: 199-208.

73. Geduldig v. Aiello, 417 U.S. 484 (1974).

74. *Id.* at 496 n.20. In 1978, the federal statute prohibiting sex discrimination in employment was amended to make pregnancy an impermissible basis for the denial of fringe benefits. 42 U.S.C. § 2000e (1976), as amended by Pub. L. No. 95-555, 92 Stat. 2076.

75. Nashville Gas Co. v. Satty, 434 U.S. 136, 142 (1977). This decision rested on a statute, but similar reasoning can be found in decisions in sex discrimination cases based on the constitutional guarantee of equal protection. See Califano v. Webster, 430 U.S. 313, 317 (1977).

76. Cleveland Board of Education v. LaFleur, 414 U.S. 632 (1974).

77. Turner v. Department of Employment Security, 423 U.S. 44, 46 (1975).

78. Susan S. Lichtendorf and Phyllis L. Gillis (1979). *The New Pregnancy*. New York: Random House.

79. Shelley E. Taylor and Ellen J. Langer (1977). "Pregnancy: a social stigma?" *Sex Roles* 3: 27-35.

80. Fred C. Pampel, Kenneth C. Land, and Marcus Felson (1977). "A social indicator model of changes in the occupational structure of the United States: 1947-1974," American Sociological Review 42: 951-964.

81. Colin Loftin and Sally K. Ward (1983). "A spatial autocorrelation model of the effects of population density on fertility," *American Sociological Review* 48:

121-128. While this study focuses on fertility, its data come from a time (1960) when induced abortion was illegal except in limited circumstances. As a result, the spatial distribution of pregnancies should not have differed from that of births.

82. Bureau of the Census, U.S. Department of Commerce (1975). *Statistical Abstract of the United States.* 96th edition. Washington, D.C.: U.S. Government Printing Office.

83. Stanley K. Henshaw and Greg Martire (1982). "Abortion and the public opinion polls. 2. Women who have had abortions," *Family Planning Perspectives* 14: 60-62.

84. Stanley K. Henshaw, Jacqueline Forrest, Ellen Sullivan, and Christopher Tietze (1982). "Abortion services in the United States, 1979 and 1980," *Family Planning Perspectives* 14: 5-15. Stanley and Kevin O'Reilly (1983). "Characteristics of abortion patients in the United States, 1979 and 1980," *Family Planning Perspectives* 15: 5-16.

85. Roe v. Wade, 410 U.S. 113 (1973).

86. Brown v. Board of Education, 347 U.S. 483 (1954).

87. 410 U.S. at 153.

88. The Court rejected the argument that human life commences at conception, an argument that, if accepted, would provide government with a compelling interest to curtail or ban access to abortion at all stages of pregnancy. However, the opinion indicates that if the question as to when life commences could be answered with certainty, the Court might respond differently to the argument. 410 U.S. at 159.

89. Evidence now exists that abortion involves a lower risk of death than carrying a pregnancy to term if it is performed prior to the sixteenth week of gestation. This is substantially later than the start of the second trimester. Willard Cates, Jr. and Christopher Tietze (1978). "Standardized mortality rates associated with legal abortion: United States, 1972-1975," *Family Planning Perspectives* 10: 109-112.

90. Simoupoulos v. Virginia, 103 S. Ct. 2532 (1983).

91. 410 U.S. at 165-166.

92. *Id.* at 165.

93. Charles F. Westoff and James McCarthy (1979). "Population attitudes and fertility," *Family Planning Perspectives* 11:93-96. L.D. Johnson, J.G. Bachman, and P.M. O'Malley (1976-1981). *Monitoring the Future.* Ann Arbor, MI.: Institute for Social Research, University of Michigan, at 82, 138, 137, 136, 138, and 139, respectively.

94. George H. Gallup (1972). *The Gallup Poll, Public Opinion: 1959-1971.* v. 3. New York: Random House.

95. Donald Granberg and Beth W. Granberg (1980). "Abortion attitudes, 1965-1980: trends and determinants," *Family Planning Perspectives* 12: 250-261 (Table 1).

96. Reprinted with permission from *id.* at 252. *Roe* itself appears to have had no influence on fertility in the United States. Timothy D. Hogan (1984). "An intervention analysis of the effects of legalized abortion upon U.S. fertility," *Population Research and Policy Review* 3 (forthcoming). This suggests that the decision of the Court was a reflection of change that had already taken place in attitudes toward abortion and childbearing.

97. This figure is the mean of the percentages of approval and of disapproval for the 1969 and two 1972 surveys.

98. *Contra* Eric M. Uslaner and Ronald E. Weber (1980). "Public support for pro-choice abortion policies in the nation and states: changes and stability after the *Roe* and *Doe* decisions," in Carl E. Schneider and Maris A. Vinoskis (eds.). *The Law and Politics of Abortion*. Lexington, MA.: D.C. Heath.

99. See, for example, Tables 1 and 2, *supra*.

100. See, for example, the section of this chapter on "Cohabitation and Contraception," *supra*.

101. "Public remains closely divided on Supreme Court's 1973 abortion ruling" (1983). *The Gallup Report*, Report No. 215: 16-18.

102. Donald Granberg (1981). "The abortion activists," *Family Planning Perspectives* 13: 157-163.

103. Granberg and Granberg, *supra* note 95, at 253-254.

104. *See id.* at 256.

105. City of Akron v. Akron Center for Reproductive Health, Inc., 103 S. Ct. 2481 (1983).

106. Planned Parenthood of Central Missouri v. Danforth, 428 U.S. 52 (1976).

107. Henshaw and O'Reilly (1983), *op. cit.*

108. 428 U.S. at 71.

109. Judith Blake (1977). "The Supreme Court's abortion decisions and public opinion in the United States," *Population and Development Review* 3: 45-62 (table 7).

110. Judith Blake and Jorge Del Pinal (1981). "Negativism, equivocation and wobbly assent: public 'support' for the prochoice platform on abortion," *Demography* 18: 309-320 (table 6).

111. Scheinberg v. Smith, 659 F.2d 476 (11th Cir. 1981).

112. *Id.* at 484.

113. *Id.*

114. The Court of Appeals remanded the case to the district court for a determination of the relationship between abortion and subsequent childbearing capacity. Research evidence indicates that women who have had an induced first-trimester abortion for their first pregnancy by vacuum aspiration (the principal method in the United States) are not, in their next pregnancy, characterized by higher rates of low birth weight, short gestation, or spontaneous abortion than women in their first pregnancy who carry that pregnancy to term. In comparing pregnancies leading to *first births*, then, it is irrelevant that the mother has had an induced first-trimester abortion by vacuum aspiration. Moreover, the ability to conceive appears to be unaffected by such abortion. However, the rates of the three problems are somewhat elevated in the second pregnancy for women who carried their first to term. Since the second pregnancy exhibits somewhat higher problem rates among women who previously aborted than among those who did not, it appears that a pregnancy carried to term offers protection to subsequent births. It is not known whether, among women aborting their first pregnancy, the first birth provides the same protection to subsequent births. Carol J. Rowland Hogue, Willard Cates, Jr. and Christopher Tietze (1983). "Impact of vacuum aspiration abortion on future childbearing: a review," *Family Planning Perspectives* 15: 119-126.

115. *The Harris Survey Yearbook of Public Opinion 1970* (1971). New York: Louis Harris & Associates, at 462.

116. George H. Gallup (1979). *The Gallup Poll, Public Opinion 1978*. Wilmington, DE.: Scholarly Resources, at 188. "Conservative social values widely held; majority wants less stress on money, more emphasis on close family ties," (1982). *The Gallup Report*, Report No. 197: 3-10.

117. "Americans at work" (1981). *Public Opinion* 4 (August/September): 21-40.

118. Wendy Baldwin and Virginia S. Cain (1980). "The children of teenage parents," *Family Planning Perspectives* 12: 34-43. Josefina J. Card (1981). "Long-term consequences for children of teenage parents," *Demography* 18: 137-156. James McCarthy and Ellen S. Radish (1982). "Education and childbearing among teenages," *Family Planning Perspectives* 14: 154-155.

119. Blake and Del Pinal, *supra* note 110, Table 6, at 317.

120. Planned Parenthood of Central Missouri v. Danforth, 428 U.S. 52 (1976).

121. Bellotti v. Baird, 443 U.S. 622 (1979).

122. City of Akron v. Akron Center for Reproductive Health, 103 S.Ct. 2481 (1983).

123. H.L. v. Matheson, 450 U.S. 398 (1981).

124. *Id.* at 410, quoting Ginsberg v. New York, 390 U.S. 629, 639 (1968).

125. Maher v. Roe, 432 U.S. 464 (1977).

126. Harris v. McRae, 448 U.S. 297 (1980).

127. *Id.* at 316-317.

128. San Antonio Independent School District v. Rodriguez, 411 U.S. 1 (1973).

129. James Trussell, Jane Menken, Barbara L. Lindheim, and Barbara Vaughan (1980). "The impact of restricting Medicaid financing for abortion," *Family Planning Perspectives* 12: 120-130.

130. The First Amendment provides in part that government "shall make no law respecting an establishment of religion."

131. Empirical evidence supporting this position appears in Donald Granberg and Beth W. Granberg, *op. cit.*, (especially Table 9); and in Henshaw and Martire (1982), *op. cit.*, (especially Table 2).

132. J. Blake (1977), *op. cit.*

133. Connie DeBoer (1977-78). "The polls: abortion," *Public Opinion Quarterly* 41: 553-564.

134. Blake and Del Pinal (1981), *op. cit.*

135. Henshaw and O'Reilly (1983), *op. cit.* (see Table 1).

136. Bureau of the Census, U.S. Department of Commerce (1980). *Statistical Abstract of the United States: 1980*. 101st edition. Washington, D.C.: U.S. Government Printing Office.

137. Anne Foner (1974). "Age stratification and age conflict in political life," *American Sociological Review* 39: 187-196 (see Table 1).

138. *Id.* at 191.

139. Cf. John Boli-Bennett and John W. Meyer (1978). "The ideology of childhood and the state: rules distinguishing children in national constitutions, 1870-1970," *American Sociological Review* 43: 797-812.

140. S. Rep. 92-26, 92nd Cong., 1st Sess., *reprinted in [1971]U.S. Code Congressional and Administrative News* 931, 934-936.

141. The Court agreed to hear *Roe v. Wade* on May 31, 1971. Oral argument took place initially on December 13, 1971, with reargument on October 11, 1972.

142. Bureau of the Census, U.S. Department of Commerce (1981). *Statistical Abstract of the United States: 1981*. Washington, D.C.: U.S. Government Printing Office.

143. For recent research on the causes of illegitimacy, see: Larry Freshnock and Phillips Cutright (1979). "Models of illegitimacy: United States, 1969," *Demography* 16: 37-47. Lynn K. White (1979). "The correlates of urban illegitimacy in the United States, 1960-1970," *Journal of Marriage and the Family* 41: 715-726. Barbara S. Janowitz (1976). "The impact of AFDC on illegitimate birth rates," *Journal of Marriage and the Family* 38: 485-494.

144. Ruth Clark and Greg Martire (1979). "Americans, still in a family way," *Public Opinion* 2: 16-19.

145. Bureau of the Census, *supra* note 142.

146. Josefina J. Card (1981), *op. cit.* Baldwin and Cain (1980), *op. cit.*

147. See John E. Nowak, Ronald D. Rotunda, and J. Nelson Young (1983). *Constitutional Law*. 2d ed. St. Paul, MN.: West.

148. George Will (1980). "The '70's, decade of second thoughts," *Public Opinion* 3: 19-43.

149. Parham v. Hughes, 441 U.S. 347, 353 (1979). *See* Plyler v. Doe, 457 U.S. 202, 219-220 (1982).

150. Bureau of the Census, U.S. Department of Commerce (1982). "Trends in child care arrangements of working mothers," *Current Population Reports*, Series P-23, No. 117.

151. Harriet B. Presser and Wendy Baldwin (1980). "Child care as a constraint on employment: prevalence, correlates, and bearing on the work and fertility nexus," *American Journal of Sociology* 85: 1202-1213.

152. Connie DeBoer (1977). "The polls: women at work," *Public Opinion Quarterly* 41: 268-277.

153. Presser and Baldwin, *supra* note 151, at 1205, 1206.

154. William Roth (1982). "The politics of day care," *Society* 19: 62-69.

155. *Id.* at 67. This reason was given by President Richard M. Nixon for his veto of the Comprehensive Child Development Act of 1971, which would have provided federal funding for day care centers for the poor.

156. J. Kagan, R.B. Kearlsey and P.B. Zelago (1977). "The effects of infant day care on psychological development," *Evaluation Quarterly* 1: 109-142.

157. Clark and Martire (1979), *op. cit.*

158. De La Cruz v. Tormey, 582 F. 2d 45 (9th Cir. 1978), *cert. denied*, 441 U.S. 965 (1979).

159. *Id.* at 64.

160. Joachim Singelmann (1978). "The sectoral transformation of the labor force in seven industrialized countries, 1920-1979," *American Journal of Sociology* 83: 1224-1234. The proportion of the labor force employed in the social service sector (specified in Table 2) rose by 5.7% between 1920 and 1930, by 8.7% between 1930 and 1940, by 24.0% between 1940 and 1950, by 31.5% between 1950 and 1960, and by 31.9% between 1960 and 1970.

161. Moshe Semyonov and Richard Scott (1983). "Industrial shifts, female employment, and occupational differentiation: a dynamic model for American cities, 1960-1970," *Demography* 20: 163-176. *See* Steven D. McLaughlin (1978), "Occupational sex identification and the assessment of male and female earnings inequality," *American Sociological Review* 43: 909-921.

162. Linda J. Waite (1976). "Working wives: 1940-1960," *American Sociological Review* 41: 65-80.

163. Seymour Spilerman (1977). "Careers, labor market structure, and socioeconomic achievement," *American Journal of Sociology* 83: 551-593.

164. *See* Mary G. Powers and Joseph J. Salvo (1982). "Fertility and child care arrangements as mechanisms of status articulation," *Journal of Marriage and the Family* 44: 21-34.
For a recent study of the attitudes of young adults toward the division of labor in childrearing, see Herzog and Bachman (1982), *op. cit.*

165. Large organizations for the delivery of social services presumably became more numerous as the result of the growth of employment for these services. Careers are associated with relatively large organizations, and in the service sector, such organizations tend to prefer female employees. William P. Bridges (1980). "Industry marginality and female employment: a new appraisal," *American Sociological Review* 45: 58-75.

166. Griswold v. Connecticut, 381 U.S. 479, 501 (1965)(Harlan, J., concurring). The Court expressly acknowledged Justic Harlan's point in Moore v. City of East Cleveland, 431 U.S. 494, 503 (1977).

Chapter III.
Mortality

We turn now to another basic demographic process — mortality — within the context of a claim of individual rights in opposition to government regulation. In considering mortality, however, we find appreciably fewer constitutional issues than existed with regard to the demographic process of fertility. The reasons for this are probably twofold. First, fertility appears to be a more complex process sociologically, involving many more causal variables than for mortality. The greater complexity can probably be attributed to the fact that fertility occurs while the lifestyle of the individual is forming; mortality, on the other hand, comes normally after a lifestyle has been well established. Second, fertility is more likely to involve competing considerations under prevailing social values. Reactions to pregnancy and children thus vary,[1] while those to death appear to be more uniform.

Nevertheless, the process of mortality is of equal import and interest in contemporary society. The 1960s and 1970s saw the dying process rise to prominence as a socially and judicially contested issue. The publication in 1969 of Elizabeth Kubler-Ross' controversial book *On Death and Dying* [2] helped focus public attention on this issue. By analyzing the stages of reaction of dying patients to their impending deaths, Kubler-Ross erased the centuries-old taboo on open discussion of death. The book capitulated the death and dying issue into the public forum.[3]

The salience of the death issue resulted from the tremendous advance of medical knowledge and technology. Infectious diseases were virtually eliminated as a cause of mortality in the United States, and rather than being instantaneous, death could now unfold in the context of chronic illness and extended medical treatment. Moreover, technological advance allowed the indefinite postponement of death in some cases. Where once the onset of dying meant a swift and sure demise, now life-support systems could keep a dying patient's heart beating and lungs breathing indefinitely. This technology created many of the moral problems that brought the life-or-death issue into the courts. The period following World War II had seen an increased emphasis on individual rights generally, and this was reflected in the death and dying issue.[4] If machines could keep a dying person alive, was that person or his/her legal guardians or next-to-kin legally obligated to accept the technologically possible prolongation of life? Thus the individual's ability to control his or her own death conflicted with the opportunity for indeterminant prolongation of life and the traditional interest of the medical profession and the State in such prolongation. The issue became whether a dying, competent individual (or the relatives of a dying incompetent individual, or minor) could refuse treatment or whether the State could intervene to require treatment.

Generally speaking, the controversy has been judicially resolved by a relatively simple principle: The right of the individual to make a death decision increases, and the strength of the State's interest in preserving life decreases, as the age and competency of the individual involved increases. The more competent, responsible and autonomous is an individual in his or her decisionmaking capacity, the stronger is the individual's right to choose not to have life unduly prolonged by heroic measures, and the less is the State's interest in intervening to prevent such a choice. Accordingly, the ability of an individual to choose death and override the State's concern with preserving life is determined by the extent to which the individual satisfies four criteria. A decision to die predominates (1)when it is free, uncoerced and intentional; (2)when it is consistent with the person's character and life plans; (3)when it is made after reasonable and knowledgeable deliberation; and (4)when it is based on moral values derived from reflection.[5] Increasingly, the courts will acquiesce to a competent adult's decision to refuse or to terminate extraordinary life-support measures when it meets all or most of these four criteria.

Strong public support exists for this position, and it has been legitimated by state legislation authorizing "durable powers of attorney" and "living wills." All but eight states in the United

States now permit persons to assign the power of attorney to a relative or other person to make life or death decisions for them with regard to treatment should they become incompetent and terminally ill. Additionally, 14 states have authorized living wills in which persons may declare while healthy that extraordinary measures should not be taken to preserve their lives in such circumstances.[6] Although there is some question as to whether living wills are legally binding, more than four out of five women surveyed in 1976 believed that they should be honored by all parties concerned, including the court, family, physician, clergy, and insurance industry.[7]

In the case of an unconscious, terminally-ill adult — who is incompetent to make an autonomous death decision — the State will cede its interest in life preservation to the wishes of the legal guardian or next-of-kin. Mentally competent relatives or guardians may make a death decision for the incompetent adult by substituting their judgment for that of the individual and making the decision on the basis of what that individual could be expected to have desired. On the other hand, as the competence of the individual declines because of youth, the State's interest increases in taking measures to preserve that individual's life. Thus for the defective newborn whose chances for ultimate survival are small and whose quality of life will be less than desirable, the State may still order extraordinary intervention in order to preserve its life. The infant does not have the capacity to protect itself or to make an autonomous life-death decision, nor has it a sufficient life history on which a surrogate could determine its wishes.[8] The State's interest in preserving the health and life of an older minor child is also strong for the same reasons.

Nonetheless, neither the State's right to preserve life in the case of an incompetent and vulnerable defective newborn nor the right of the lucid and competent person to make a death choice is absolute. Under current public policy, the individual does not have the right to require the State or the medical profession to preserve his or her life at all costs, nor is there an absolute right on the part of the competent individual to be killed or to kill himself or herself. The extremes lie outside the constitutional umbrella. Thus, in some cases defective newborns have been allowed to die, and there has never been a right to active euthanasia and suicide. The individual possesses constitutional rights only where permitting death would be generally regarded as a humanitarian act.[9] Such a situation may exist in the case of the terminally and painfully ill adult, the unconscious and vegetative person, or the grossly deformed infant.

Alternatively, the right-to-die in these instances may simply be an extension of the right to life guaranteed by the Fifth and Fourteenth Amendments. According to this view, the Founding Fathers meant the right to life, along with the basic rights to liberty and property, to be discretionary rather than mandatory. Citizens are regarded as autonomous persons who may choose to exercise or to waive basic rights, or to exercise them in one way rather than another. A citizen has "the right to be one's own master, to dispose of one's own lot as one chooses," the right to decide to "come or go,... to read or not read, to speak or not speak, to worship or not worship, to buy, sell or sit tight...." So, too, the citizen has the right to exercise the right to life by forgoing it and choosing death.[10]

The point of controversy is where to draw the dividing line between constitutional protection and nonprotection. At the present time, it is generally placed between passive and active euthanasia. The competent person, and the family or guardian on behalf of the voiceless individual, may passively acquiesce to approaching death, but they may not personally engage in conduct that terminates a painful or hopeless life or promote such conduct by medical personnel or others. The competent, terminally-ill adult can be allowed to die (passive euthanasia), but (s)he has no legal right to insist that others cause her death at a certain time (active euthanasia or mercy killing) or to take her own life (suicide). Similarly, the family or legal guardian can make a decision in favor of passive euthanasia for the incompetent adult, but active euthanasia is not permissible.

However, because of the ambiguity surrounding the distinction between active and passive euthanasia, and because public attitudes appear to be increasingly supportive of active as well as passive euthanasia, it is possible that the courts will move the dividing line and include constitutional protection for active euthanasia at least under some conditions. Along these lines, it may be argued that the courts should take the position that the motive behind the intervention should determine whether euthanasia is permissible, and not whether the intervention is active or passive.

If the motive is humanitarian, then it may be equally permissible to end a suffering, terminally ill patient's life actively or passively. In fact, active euthanasia may be more humanitarian than passive intervention because it relieves and shortens suffering.[11]

1. Court Decisions: Children

Turning to court decisions, perhaps the best known cases are those in which parents have desired to withhold treatment from seriously deformed newborn infants. While there seems to be widespread judicial and public agreement concerning the right to die of competent adults, there is disagreement concerning whether medical treatment should be withheld from newborns with severe birth defects. Three types of defects are most common: Down's syndrome, which is often accompanied by intestinal blockages that require surgery to allow nourishment to be taken; spina bifida, which requires surgery to close spinal lesions that are subject to life-threatening infection; and extreme prematurity, which is accompanied by chronic and life-threatening lung disease.[12] The issue of how infants born with these conditions should be treated was placed on the public agenda in 1973 when two physicians disclosed that 14 per cent of infant deaths in their intensive-care pediatric clinic had resulted from withholding or suspending medical treatment.[13] Subsequent to this disclosure, judicial and professional opinion polarized and solidified. Some argued that humane treatment for the deformed infant consists in withholding medical treatment when the infant's suffering is prolonged and unrelievable, when the treatment itself will contribute to the infant's suffering rather than alleviate it, when the probability of survival beyond a few days or months is low, and when the infant has little hope for even minimally enjoyable or meaningful "life experiences" in the interim.[14] Under such circumstances it would be in the child's "best interest"[15] to withhold treatment since treatment would simply prolong suffering and dying rather than preserve life.[16] In a recent survey of New Haven pediatricians, there was virtually unanimous approval of passive euthanasia in such cases.[17]

In 1982, the Indiana Supreme Court followed this logic when it permitted the parents of a seriously deformed and retarded newborn to refuse corrective surgery for an esophagus blockage which prevented the infant from taking nourishment. No food or water was given intraveneously, and the baby died six days after birth while state officials were seeking a hearing before the U.S. Supreme Court to overrule the state court ruling.[18] Slightly more than a year after this ruling, a slim plurality (43%) favored this "Baby Doe" decision.[19] However, most courts will approve requests by hospitals and order extraordinary intervention over the objection of the parents even when faced with a situation that involves unrelievable suffering, treatment contributing to suffering, a low quality of life, and a negative prognosis for ultimately successful treatment. Such decisions have been made in at least several instances involving severe birth defects.[20]

When illness or injury is involved, there also appears to be little question that the state can intervene if it chooses. A temporary guardian can be appointed by a court to consent to medical treatment (e.g., blood transfusions) for the child even though the treatment violates the family's religion and the free exercise of religion as an express constitutional guarantee.[21] A woman pregnant with a viable fetus can be required to undergo surgery and accept a blood transfusion in violation of her religion if such is needed to preserve the life of the child.[22] There is also no justifiable basis for objections to government-enforced medical treatment from the constitutional right of parents to raise their children;[23] courts may overrule the right when the health of the child is in jeopardy. Indeed, State intervention is permissible not only for children facing death but for children whose condition is serious but less than life-threatening.[24]

> [T]he parental right to control a child's nurture is grounded not in any absolute property right which can be enforced to the detriment of the child, but rather is akin to a trust, subject to a correlative duty to care for and protect the child, and terminable by the parents' failure to discharge their obligations[25]

This view is consistent with and may reflect increasing public protection that has been given children in nations generally during the past century.[26] The trend has been explained sociologically as the result of the growth of both individualism and the progress-seeking nation-state. The individual, rather than a group such as the family, has come to be viewed as the source of progress, a goal deemed central to the nation-state. These ideological changes have required the welfare and potential of children to be brought increasingly under the purview of the political institutions of society.[27]

Parental rights nonetheless remain strong. Even in the face of a life-threatening illness in a child, parents have the ability to select a course of treatment that, while not viewed favorably by the medical community, is administered by a physician licensed by the State and reasonable under the circumstances. Thus, a State cannot prevent the parents of a child suffering from Hodgkins disease from placing the child under the care of a physician who administers a nonconventional form of treatment (nutritional therapy) where there is evidence the child is improving under it and reasonable concern exists over the side-effects of conventional treatments (radiation and chemotherapy).[28] However, parental rights extend beyond the ability to consent to nonconventional forms of medical treatment that have a reasonable potential to help their child; they also provide parents with the ability to consent to conventional forms that may entail some risk to a healthy sibling. Parents can agree — though at this time only with court approval — to the removal of a kidney from one of their children for transplantation into another; this may be done in order to save the life of the latter where the procedure carries a high likelihood of success for the recipient and only a minimal risk to the physical health of the donor.[29] Because "the filial bond is one of the strongest, yet most delicate, and most inviolable of all relationships,"[30] State deference to parental judgments is constitutionally required unless a clear threat exists to their child's health.

2. Court Decisions: Adults

With regard to life-threatening conditions involving adults, we find considerable constitutional resistance to enforced medical treatment and widespread public support for a constitutional "right to die." Mentally competent adults possess the right — though it is not absolute in nature — to opt against treatment even if death is likely to ensue. Appellate courts have usually acknowledged that adults may refuse blood transfusions for religious reasons as long as they are cognizant of the imminence of death and as long as death will not jeopardize the well-being of the remaining members of the family.[31]

> The place of religion in our society is an exalted one, achieved through a long tradition of reliance on the home, the church, and the inviolable citadel of the individual heart and mind. We have come to recognize through bitter experience that it is not within the power of government to invade that citadel, whether its purpose or effect be to aid or oppose, to advance or retard. In the relationship between man and religion, the State is firmly committed to a position of neutrality.[32]

At the same time that the constitutional guarantee of freedom of religious exercise allows an adult to decline treatment that will save his/her life, the right of privacy permits that decision in the absence of religious considerations where death is highly probable in the near future even with treatment. For example, a Florida court allowed treatment to be discontinued for a 73-year-old man suffering from a terminal muscular disease who had physically deteriorated to the point where a respirator was needed to keep him alive — a respirator that could prolong his life for just a short period of time, and then only at the price of continued suffering.[33] In full possession of his mental faculties, he asked that the respirator be removed, arguing that continuation of enforced medical treatment was an unconstitutional intrusion into the protected realm of personal autonomy. The court agreed, evidently reflecting the view that

> The constitutional right to privacy, as we conceive it, is an expression of the sanctity of individual free choice and self-determination as fundamental constituents of life. The value of life as so perceived is lessened not by a decision to refuse treatment, but by the failure to allow a competent human being the right of choice.[34]

In making these decisions the courts have reflected the trend in public sentiment. In 1973, three out of five Americans supported a terminally ill adult's right to refuse or suspend life-prolonging medical treatment; by 1981, support had grown to four out of five. Table 3-1 displays the upward trend in public support for the individual's "right to die."

A second aspect of the "right to die" issue concerns the ability of family members to have life-support systems discontinued for comatose and terminally ill patients. Here, the right of privacy allows the person who is in an irreversible vegetative state to avoid the extensive treatment needed to prevent death when the family of the person so chooses. The public interest in preserving life

Table 3-1. The Individual's Right-To-Die (U. S.)

Question	Answer	1973	1977	1981
Do you think a patient with a terminal disease ought to be able to tell his doctor to let him die rather than to extend his life when no cure is in sight, or do you think this is wrong?	Let die	62%	71%	78%
	Wrong	28%	18%	19%
	Not sure	10%	11%	3%
		100%	100%	100%

SOURCE: Louis Harris (1981). "Terminally ill should have right to die." *The Harris Survey*, May 14: 1-2.

declines and the right of privacy increases in proportion to the degree of bodily invasion required by the treatment and the likelihood that treatment cannot restore some semblance of normal health.[35]

> The notion that the individual exists for the good of the state is, of course, quite antithetical to our fundamental thesis that the role of the state is to ensure a maximum of individual freedom of choice and conduct.[36]

The judicial resolution of this "Quinlan Question" has the overwhelming support of the American public. In 1977, a year after the New Jersey Supreme Court allowed Karen Quinlan to be taken off a respirator at the request of her parents, two-thirds of the public agreed with this course of action. In 1981, almost three-fourths of the public approved suspension of life-prolonging treatment for terminally ill and comatose patients at the request of the family.[37]

The individual's "right to die" and the right of the family to refuse or suspend life-prolonging measures for the comatose, terminally ill patient are related to the issue of active euthanasia. Public attitudes on the issue were ascertained as early as 1937 and have been regularly sampled since that time. In the late 1930s, almost half of those surveyed approved of "mercy deaths under government supervision for hopeless invalids." Since then, support for mercy killing has reached the point where approximately three out of five Americans now give their approval. The percentages of those who approved and disapproved of active euthanasia at various points between 1937 and 1983 are shown in Table 3-2. It should be noted that in the case of the second and third questions in this table, comparisons of public opinion are possible over a substantial period of time. On both questions, marked increases in approval were registered.

Approval or disapproval by the public of the individual's "right to die," of the family's suspension of life support for the comatose and terminally ill patient, and of active euthanasia for the painfully and terminally ill patient — that is, support of the death options — is related to a number of demographic characteristics.

The most striking relationship is an apparent correlation between increasing age and disapproval of the death options. This apparent relationship can be illustrated with data from three separate surveys conducted during the 1970s. Two of the surveys dealt with active euthanasia, while the third asked a question which combined the "right to die" and Quinlan situations. Table 3-3 presents the results.

However, the apparent relationship between age and death option attitudes can be explained by other factors. When a control is introduced for attitudes toward individual rights — as measured by whether respondents support the right of free speech for communists, atheists and militants,[38] by whether respondents believe generally that a patient has a right to make a medical treatment decision in opposition to physicians' recommendations, and by whether respondents themselves have deviated from recommended treatment in the past[39] — the relationship between age and death attitudes disappears. The more people believe generally in individual rights, especially with regard to patient's rights, the more likely they are to approve of the death options, and their age disappears as an explanatory factor. Similarly, religious intensity — as measured by frequency of church attendance and degree of religious commitment — also dissolves the apparent relationship between age and disapproval of the death options. As religiosity increases, approval of death decisions falls.[40]

3. Religious Beliefs and Affiliation

The philosophy of American society with regard to death, including that manifest in court decisions, apparently stems in significant measure from religious philosophy. It is thus noteworthy

Table 3-2. Public Attitudes Toward Active Euthanasia (United States)

Question		1937	1939	YEAR: 1947	1950	1973*	1977*	1981	1983
Do you favor mercy killing under gov't supervision for hopeless invalids?	Yes	46%a	46%a						
	No	54%	54%						
		100%	100%						
When a person has an incurable disease, do you think doctors should be allowed by law to end the patient's life by some painless means if the patient and his family request it?	Yes			37%a	43%b	53%c	60%d		63%e
	No			54%	46%	40%	36%		33%
	No opinion			9%	11%	7%	4%		4%
				100%	100%	100%	100%		100%
Do you think the terminally ill patient, with no cure in sight, ought to have the right to tell his doctor to put him out of his misery, or do you think this is wrong?	Ought to be allowed					37%f	49%f	56%f	
	This is wrong					53%	38%	41%	
	Not sure					10%	13%	3%	
						100%	100%	100%	

* The wording of the two 1973 questions and the two 1977 questions seems to be related to the difference between them in approval levels of euthanasia. The last (Harris) question may show a lower level because it asks the respondent to approve only on the strength of the patient's request and does not include the additional support of the family in the request, as does the middle (Gallup-NORC) question. Further, the last (Harris) question asks only if euthanasia should be legal. Respondents consistently agree to the legalization of such practices as abortion and euthanasia in greater numbers than they approve of the morality of the practices. This merely indicates that the public would not legally deny to others what it does not morally approve for itself.

SOURCES: (a) George H. Gallup (1972). *The Gallup Poll, Public Opinion 1935-1971*, v. 1, *1935-1948*. New York: Random House, at 46, 131, 656.
(b) George H. Gallup (1972). *The Gallup Poll, Public Opinion 1935-1971*, v. 2, *1949-1958*. New York: Random House, at 887.
(c) George H. Gallup (1978). *The Gallup Poll, Public Opinion 1972-1977*, v. 1, *1972-1975*. Wilmington, DE.: Scholarly Resources, at 143.
(d) National Opinion Research Center (1982). *General Social Surveys, 1972-1982: Cumulative Codebook*. Chicago: University of Chicago, at 165.
(e) National Opinion Research Center (1983). *General Social Surveys, 1972-1983: Cumulative Codebook*. Chicago: University of Chicago, at 183.
(f) Louis Harris (1981). "Terminally ill should have right to die," *The Harris Survey*, May 14: 1-2.

Table 3-3. Relationship between Age and Disapproval of the Death Options

Question	1973 % re- plying yes		1976 % disagree & strongly disagree		1977 % re- plying yes	
Euthanasia: When a person has an incurable disease, do you think doctors should be allowed by law to end the patient's life by some painless means if the patient and his family request it?*	Under 30 30-49 yrs 50 yrs.+	67% 51% 44%				
Right to die and Quinlan Question: When a person is in the last stages of a terminal illness, the patient or his family should decide if further treatment should be continued.**			Under 35 35-49 yrs 50-64 yrs 65 yrs.+	12% 13% 14% 23%		
Euthanasia: Do you think doctors should be allowed by law to end a patient's life by some painless means if an incurably ill patient and his family request it?***					18-25 yrs. 26-34 yrs. 35-44 yrs. 45-54 yrs. 55-64 yrs. 65 yrs.+	72% 68% 60% 61% 59% 54%

SOURCES: * George H. Gallup (1978). *The Gallup Poll, Public Opinion 1972-1977,* v. 1, *1972-1975.* Wilmington, DE.: Scholarly Resources, at 143.
  ** Marie Haug (1978). "Aging and the right to terminate medical treatment," *Journal of Gerontology* 33: 586-591.
  *** B. K. Singh (1979). "Correlates of attitudes toward euthanasia," *Social Biology* 26: 247-254.

that religious affiliation appears to have little direct influence on death option attitudes. Catholics and Protestants approve of the death options in about equal numbers.[41] This appears to reflect the lack of clear-cut differences between the major religious groups in formal philosophy relevant to the issue.

The Roman Catholic Church takes a definitive three-fold position with regard to the treatment of the terminally and painfully ill:

It condemns active euthanasia; it requires the use of ordinary means to preserve life; and it permits withholding or suspending extraordinary means of medical treatment.

According to the Roman Catholic Church, active euthanasia is never permissible.[42] But euthanasia can also be passive, the omission of required acts, and here a distinction exists between ordinary and extraordinary means of medical treatment. Ordinary means of medical treatment are those which "offer a reasonable hope of benefit for the patient and can be obtained and used without excessive pain, expense, or other inconveniences."[43] Omission of the ordinary means of care is also considered euthanasia. Both active euthanasia and omission of ordinary care constitute "crime[s] against life, and an attack on humanity." They violate the right to life and "the dignity of the human person." They also violate "the divine law"[44] which gives God "supreme dominion over His creatures"[45] and allows God rather than man to determine the point of death for each person.

However, extraordinary means of treatment are never required. Extraordinary means may be refused or allowed at the discretion of the patient, family and doctors.[46] Extraordinary means are those treatment methods which involve "excessive pain" or "expense," which do "not offer a reasonable hope of benefit,"[47] which "impose on the patient strain or suffering out of proportion with the benefits," or which are experimental.[48]

The Roman Catholic Church's position on euthanasia, particularly its endorsement of the refusal and suspension of extraordinary life-support measures, is based on several doctrines of Christian faith. These include the doctrines of original sin, the immortality of the soul, and the resurrection of the body.

According to the doctrine of original sin, when Adam, the first man, sinned, he separated himself from God and brought the punishment of death upon himself and the entire human race, of which he was the progenitor. Death is "the consequence of sin," a necessary suffering and ultimate evil that all humanity must endure and conquer in order to atone for individual and universal sin. Extraordinary attempts to avoid death interfere with the natural unfolding of the supernatural experience and meaning of death.[49] Although not forbidden, they are also not required.

The doctrines of the immortality of the soul and the resurrection of the body add a further dimension to the meaning of death.

Earthly death is not final, but a mere separation of the soul and body.[50] The soul lives on and is immortal and eternal. Eventually, just as Jesus Christ triumphed over sin and death by rising from the dead, so too all human beings will rise at the Last Judgment. Bodies and souls will be reunited for eternal life,[51] and this provides an other-worldly meaning that removes the horror and finality of earthly death. Because death is not the "total extinction" of life,[52] extraordinary means need not be taken to support the present form of life. Earthly death need not be desparately avoided, and earthly life need not be needlessly prolonged.

Other Christian denominations are divided over the ideas of immortality of the soul and euthanasia.[53] However, there is a strong American Protestant tradition dating from the early days of the Pilgrims and Puritans that life on earth is a pilgrimage or transition to eternal life.[54] Thus, the proportion of Catholics who believe in life after death has not been markedly different from the proportion of Protestants holding this belief over the past 30 years.[55] Significantly, the afterlife is viewed as an improved state compared to earthly life. When asked to describe how life after death will differ, the most frequent responses of the seven out of ten Americans who are believers were that there would be "no more problems or troubles," that the afterlife would be "better," "peaceful," and "happy," without "sickness," "pain," or "sorrow."[56]

The Christian doctrines of the immortality of the soul and the resurrection of the body had their philosophical origins in the ancient Greek philosophers rather than the Hebrew tradition. With regard to the latter, the Old Testament and Judaic conceptions of death held that earthly death is final. If immortality existed at all, it resided in the continuance of the Jewish people in history rather than in personal survival.[57] Modern Judaism is divided concerning immortality of the soul, with some segments retaining the Old Testament interpretation and others adopting variants of the Christian dogma.[58] The differences in views regarding the meaning of death between Christian and Judaic traditions are reflected in differences of opinion on euthanasia between their adherents. Jews consistently approve of euthanasia in greater numbers than either Protestants or Catholics.[59] This difference seems anomalous. One would expect that Christians, since they anticipate an afterlife, would be more willing to accept euthanasia and the end of earthly life than Jews, who anticipate an afterlife in far smaller numbers.[60] However, the reverse is true. It is an anomaly for which no clear explanation exists.

4. A Final Distinction

Government insistence upon a form of medical treatment for an adult is to be distinguished from the refusal of government to allow access to a particular type of treatment. A requirement that the individual facing death pursue a certain course encounters an obstacle in the right of privacy, but that right does not allow even the terminally ill individual to force government to make available a type of treatment the safety and effectiveness of which is unclear.[61] The interest in protecting the public from unknown medical treatments is strong, and their prohibition does not infringe the right of privacy to a sufficient degree that government is forced to demonstrate more than a reasonable basis for its position. Government and the individual thus operate within separate spheres, and in the context of medical treatment for life-threatening conditions, each possesses barriers to coercion by the other. However, restrictions on items of questionable medical efficacy are not necessarily popular with the general public. In the late 1970s, the Food and Drug Administration banned a drug (laetrile) that was thought by some to be effective in treating cancer, but a clear majority of Americans opposed the action and favored state legalization of it in spite of the federal policy.[62]

5. Conclusion

By way of conclusion, the societal context in which the legal developments occurred must not be overlooked. While technological advance made possible the extension of life, the greater frequency of public questioning of the desirability of such extention would not have materialized during the 1970s unless there was a societal inclination to examine the issue. Changing technology provided the opportunity for the questions to arise, but the operation of social factors was critical in encouraging their emergence and referral to the courts. What were those factors? It is this question that we now examine.

One probable factor promoting the questions and their judicial resolution was a decline in commonly-held values in American society between 1940 and 1970.[63] With lessened commitment to identifiable, shared goals and standards, the likelihood was enhanced that there would be resort to the judiciary, for with an eroded base of accepted values, uncertainty will exist with regard to a course of action on important social issues such as whether to extend life. In the face of uncertainty, it is logical to expect the officially-sanctioned agency for the resolution of controversies to be employed. In short, the increased number of court decisions during the 1970s on the question of the "right to die" reflected to some extent deterioration in moral integration. That deterioration appears paradoxically to have been caused in appreciable measure by population growth.[64]

A second probable factor promoting questions regarding the desirability of life-prolonging medical technology was an intensified examination by Americans of their quality of life, an examination that may have resulted from a declining commitment to the value of productive efficiency.[65] The use of medical technology was evidently scrutinized as part of a broad reexamination by Americans of the priorities of their society.[66] The environmental movement reflected this fundamental philosophical reexamination; it is not accidental that support for the movement rose rapidly between 1968 and 1970.[67] An emphasis upon personal fulfillment rather than economic productivity developed as the central theme of a trend that had its inception in the 1960s. In the words of an extensive study of American public opinion:

> A new synthesis is forming, one that meshes three elements: the pursuit of economic stability (even at the cost of reduced consumption) with more modest material expectations and with the drive to establish maximum control over one's own destiny.[68]

NOTES

1. Among once-married American women, one out of three pregnancies is viewed negatively or with mixed feelings. The same proportion is terminated by abortion. Charles F. Westoff (1980). "Women's reactions to pregnancy," *Family Planning Perspectives* 12: 135-139. Stanley K. Henshaw and Kevin O'Reilly (1983). "Characteristics of abortion patients in the United States, 1979 and 1980," *Family Planning Perspectives* 15: 5-16.

2. Elizabeth Kubler-Ross (1969). *On Death and Dying*. New York: Macmillan.

3. Renee C. Fox (1981). "The sting of death in American society," *Social Service Review* 55: 42-59.

4. *Id.* at 43-45, 55.

5. Bruce C. Miller (1981). "Autonomy and the refusal of life saving treatment," *Hastings Center Report* 11: 22-28.

6. John J. Lombard, James L. Miller, Ronald E. Gather, and Rodney D. Houghton (1978). "Legal problems of the aged and infirm - the durable power of attorney - planned protective services and the living will," *Real Estate, Probate and Trust Journal* 13: 1-67.

7. "Pulling the plug: Is it murder or mercy?" *Ladies Home Journal* 93 (March, 1976): 98-99.

8. John A. Robertson (1982). "Legal aspects of withholding medical treatment from handicapped children," in A.E. Doudera and J. Douglas Peters (eds.) *Legal and Ethical Aspects of Treating Critically and Terminally Ill Patients*. Ann Arbor, MI.: Aupha Press.

9. Peter C. Williams (1977). "Rights and the alleged right of innocents to be killed," *Ethics* 87: 383-394.

10. Joel Fineberg (1978). "Voluntary euthanasia and the inalienable right to life," *Philosophy & Public Affairs* 7: 93-123. Quotation from p. 121; copyright 1977 by the Tanner Lecture Trust.

11. James Rachels (1975). "Active and passive euthanasia," *New England Journal of Medicine* 292:78-80.

12. Albert R. Jonsen (1982). "Ethics, the law, and the treatment of the seriously ill newborn," in Doudera and Peters, *op. cit.*

13. Raymond S. Duff and A.G.M. Campbell (1973). "Moral and ethical dilemmas in the special care nursery," *New England Journal of Medicine* 289: 890-894.

14. Robertson (1982), *op. cit.*, note 12.

15. Judith P. Swazey (1981). "Treatment and nontreatment decisions: in whose best interests?" in Cynthia B. Wong and Judith P. Swazey (eds.), *Dilemmas of Dying*. Boston: G.K. Hall.

16. Thelma Schorr (1976). "The right to die," *American Journal of Nursing* 76: 53.

17. Raymond S. Duff and A.G.M. Campbell (1980). "Moral and ethical dilemmas seven years into the debate about human ambiguity," *Annals of the American Academy of Political Science* 447: 19-28.

18. Fred Barbash and Christine Russell. "The demise of 'infant' Doe," *Washington Post*, April 17, 1982 at A1, A10.

19. "Public evenly divided on whether deformed infants should be kept alive or allowed to die" (1983), *Gallup Report,* Report No. 213: 11-12.

20. *Maine Medical Center v. Houle*, Civil No. 74-145 (Super Ct. Cumberland County, Feb. 14, 1974). Robert and Peggy Stinson (1979). "On the death of a baby," *Atlantic Monthly* 244: 64-72. Jay Mathews. "Brian: another side in the debate over severe birth defects," *Washington Post*, May 21, 1982, at A1, A18.

21. Jehovah's Witnesses v. King County Hospital, 278 F. Supp. 488 (W.D. Washington 1967) (three-judge court), *aff'd*, 390 U.S. 598 (1968). *Accord*, People In the Interest of D.L.E., 645 P.2d 271 (Colo. 1982).

22. Jefferson v. Griffin Spalding County Hospital Authority, 247 Ga. 86, 274 S.E.2d 457 (1981).

23. Custody of a Minor, 379 N.E.2d 1053 (Mass. 1978). *See generally* Santosky v. Kramer, 102 S. Ct. 1388 (1982).

24. In re Karwath, 199 N.W.2d 900, 278 N.E.2d 918 (1972). *Contra*, In re Green, 448 Pa. 338, 292 A.2d 387 (1972).

25. Custody of a Minor, 393 N.E.2d 836, 843 (Mass. 1979).

26. John Boli:Bennett and John W. Meyer (1978). "The ideology of childhood and the state: rules distinguishing children in national constitutions, 1870-1970," *American Sociological Review* 43: 797-812.

27. *Id.*

28. In the Matter of Hofbauer, 47 N.Y.2d 648, 393 N.E.2d 1009 (1979).

29. Little v. Little, 576 S.W.2d 493 (Texas Ct. Civ. App. 1979); Hart v. Brown, 289 A.2d 386 (Conn. Super. Ct. 1972).

30. In the Matter of Hofbauer, 393 N.E.2d at 1013.

31. In the Matter of Osborne, 294 A.2d 372 (D.C. Ct. App. 1972); In re Estate of Brooks, 32 Ill. 361, 205 N.E.2d 435 (1965). *But see* John F. Kennedy Memorial Hospital v. Heston, 58 N.J. 576, 279 A.2d 670 (1971).

32. In re Estate of Brooks, 205 N.E.2d 435, 441 (Ill. 1965), quoting the U.S. Supreme Court in School District of Abington Township v. Schempp, 374 U.S. 203, 226 (1963).

33. Satz v. Perlmutter, 362 So.2d 160 (Fla. Dist. Ct. App. 1978), *aff'd*, 379 So.2d 359 (Fla. 1980). *Accord*, In the Matter of Spring, 405 N.E.2d 115 (Mass. 1980).

34. Superintendent of Belchertown State School v. Saikewicz, 373 Mass. 728, 370 N.E.2d 417, 426 (1977).

35. In the Matter of Quinlan, 70 N.J. 10, 355 A.2d 647 (1976), *cert. denied*, 429 U.S. 922 (1976).

36. In the Matter of Osborne, 294 A.2d 372, 375 n. 5 (D.C. Ct. App. 1972).

37. Louis Harris (1981). "Terminally ill should have right to die," *Harris Survey*, May 14: 1-2.

38. B.K. Singh (1979). "Correlates of attitudes toward euthanasia," *Social Biology* 26: 247-254.

39. Marie Haug (1978). "Aging and the right to terminate medical treatment," *Journal of Gerontology* 33: 586-591.

40. Singh, *supra* note 38, at 249.

41. *Id.*

42. Sacred Congregation for the Doctrine of the Faith [of the Catholic Church] (1980). "Declaration on euthanasia," in President's Commission for the Study of Ethical Problems in Medicine and Biomedical Research (1983). *Deciding to Forego Life-Sustaining Treatment*. Washington, D.C.: U.S. Government Printing Office, at 300-307.

43. Edward J. Leadem (1976). "Brief for New Jersey Catholic Conference, Amicus Curiae," in *In the Matter of Karen Ann Quinlan*. v. 2. Arlington, VA.: University Publications of America, at 197-207; quotation from p. 202.

44. Sacred Congregation, *supra* note 42, at 303.

45. Leadem, *supra* note 43, at 200.

46. Sacred Congregation, *supra* note 42, at 306.

47. Leadem, *supra* note 43, at 202.

48. Sacred Congregation, *supra* note 42, at 306.

49. Karl Rahner (1961). *On the Theology of Death*. New York: Herder and Herder, at 33, 47, 54.

50. *Id.* at 16.

51. Nicholas Berdyaev (1977). "Death and immortality," in Robert Kastenbaum (ed.), *Death as a Speculative Theme in Religious, Scientific, and Social Thought*. New York: Arno Press, at 317-337.

52. A. Roy Eckardt (1973). "Death in the Judaic and Christian traditions," in Arien Mack (ed.), *Death in the American Experience*. New York: Schocken Books, at 123-148.

53. *Id.* at 131-132.

54. Peter Smith (1961). *The American Pilgrimage*. New York: Collier Books, at 18-24.

55. George Gallup, Jr. (1982). *Adventures in Immortality*. New York: McGraw-Hill, at 184, 212.

56. *Id.* at 184.

57. Berdyaev, *supra* note 51, at 326.

58. Eckardt, *supra* note 52, at 142-143.

59. John M. Ostheimer (1980). "The polls: changing attitudes toward euthanasia," *Public Opinion Quarterly* 44: 123-128.

60. Gallup, *supra* note 55, at 212.

61. Rutherford v. United States, 616 F.2d 455 (10th Cir. 1980), *cert. denied*, 449 U.S. 937 (1980); People v. Privitera, 153 Cal. Rptr. 431, 591 P.2d 919 (1979), *cert. denied*, 444 U.S. 949 (1979).

62. Louis Harris (1977). "Laetrile ban opposed," *Harris Survey*, June 27.

63. Robert C. Angell (1974). "The moral integration of American cities. II," *American Journal of Sociology* 80: 607-629.

64. *Id. See also* Myron Boor (1981). "Relationship of 1977 state suicide rates to population increases and immigration," *Psychological Reports* 49: 856-858.

65. Richard L. Simpson (1972). "Beyond rational bureaucracy: changing values and social integration in post-industrial society," *Social Forces* 51: 1-6.

66. *See* Daniel Yankelovich and Bernard Lefkowitz (1980). "The public debate on growth: preparing for resolution," *Technological Forecasting and Social Change* 17: 95-140.

67. Kenneth E. Hornback (1974). *Orbits of Opinion: The Role of Age in the Environmental Movement's Attentive Public, 1968-1972*. Unpublished Ph.D. dissertation, Michigan State University. While there was a decline in support between 1970 and 1972, one cannot expect continued attention to a single specific issue. The underlying philosophical redirection of society will be manifested in different problems at different times.

68. Reprinted by permission from Yankelovich and Lefkowitz, *supra* note 66, at 130. Copyright 1979, and awarded the Mitchell Prize, by the Woodlands Conference.

Chapter IV.
Migration and Population Distribution

Geographic mobility is one of the most notable attributes of modern American society. Apart from the substantial daily migration that exists in commuting to and from places of employment,[1] there is considerable movement that is more permanent in nature. Almost half of all Americans between the ages of 25 and 64 changed their residence at least once between 1975 and 1980.[2] While a majority of the movers remained in the same county, more than 21 million Americans relocated in a different county and/or in a different state. Table 4-1 provides a general picture of the extent and nature of this migration.[3]

Table 4-1. Distribution of Americans 25-64 Years of Age According to Whether They Moved to A Different Home between 1975 and 1980 and the Destination of Movers

Same House, 1975-1980 (non-movers)			53%
Different house in 1980 than in 1975 (movers):			
Same state			
Same county	26%		
Different county	11%		
Total moving within state	37%	37%	
Different state		10%	
Total moving		47%	47%
		Total:	100%

The dimensions of spatial mobility reflected in the figures in Table 4-1 are impressive. During the 1970s, the movement of population represented by the figures had two significant characteristics. First, the earlier nationwide trend of the nineteenth and twentieth centuries of migration from rural areas to the cities was reversed. For the first time in the nation's history, the rate of nonmetropolitan growth exceeded that of metropolitan areas. This turnaround of the migration stream was partially related to the suburbanization trend which had begun as early as the 1930s and which accelerated greatly in the late 1950s and the 1960s.[4] Metropolitan residents who became economically established and attained enabling levels of affluence fled the physical and social deterioration of the cities for the newer housing, quieter streets, open spaces, and relative safety of the suburbs. Thus, while metropolitan areas continued to gain in population, central cities began to experience numerical declines with the quickening of suburbanization.

Demetropolitanization is partially attributable to a continuance and extension of suburbanization to ever-greater distances from the central cities. Rural counties adjacent to metropolitan areas and within commuting distance of the urban center account for a substantial proportion of nonmetropolitan growth. However, counties not adjacent to metropolitan areas have grown at virtually the same rate as adjacent counties.[5] Thus while the migration pattern up to mid-century was predominantly from farm to city to suburb, the more recent pattern was from city *and* suburb to nonmetropolitan areas. This shift in the pattern of internal U.S. migration had reflected changed public preferences for places to reside. Table 4-2 indicates that early in the 1970s the largest proportion of Americans preferred to live in small towns, but in 1977, the largest percentage (almost four in ten persons) preferred rural areas.

Table 4-2. Preference for Place of Residence (United States)

Year	Proportion Preferring			
	City	Suburb	Small Town	Farm/Rural Area
1970	18	26	31	24
1971	17	26	31	25
1972	13	31	32	23
1977	13	29	20	38

SOURCE: "The 70's, decade of second thoughts," *Public Opinion* 3 (December/January 1980): 19-43; p. 35 (data from surveys by the Gallup organization).

The second significant trend in migration in the 1970s was movement from the industrial areas of the northeastern and north-central regions to the so-called sunbelt, i.e., the South and West. This trend, too, represented a turnaround of the earlier pattern of migration. Although it was a distinct phenomenon, the trend was related to the nonmetropolitan-metropolitan reversal. The industrial revolution of the nineteenth century triggered the mass movement of rural southerners to the industrial cities of the North in search of economic opportunity, a migration flow which persisted into the 1960s. The 1970s saw a reversal of this trend, with industries and people leaving the energy- and employment-poor cities of the North for the better labor markets, cheaper energy costs, wider spaces, and milder climates of the newer cities and nonurbanized areas which abound in the sunbelt.[6] Cities and rural areas of the sunny South and West held greater attractiveness for fulfilling lives than did the economically depressed urban centers of the cold North. The north-south stream thus was a correlative aspect of the urban-to-rural deconcentration which predominated in all areas of the country.[7] People left the cities for rural areas, and left particularly the cities of the North for the generally more-rural South and West, for many of the same reasons.[8]

Although environmental and noneconomic reasons for migration were growing in importance in the 1970s, and economic factors may have declined in influence,[9] economic motivations still continued to predominate. More than half of those who changed their state of residence in the mid-1970s moved primarily for employment-related reasons, with locational and quality-of-life considerations secondary. In terms of the latter, the reason for moving cited most often after job-related motives was to be closer to relatives.[10]

That individual households are moving to nonmetropolitan areas and the sunbelt primarily for employment-related rather than quality of life considerations only partially explains the migration phenomenon. People may be moving to jobs in less urbanized places and warmer climates because of the prior movement of firms. Jobs may be increasingly located outside northern industrialized metropolitan areas because land is cheaper and more abundant, the climate is more favorable, the costs of labor and energy are less,[11] and improved communication and transportation systems permit business to be conducted at greater distances from urban centers.[*12*]

Public policies also promoted de-urbanization. The construction of the interstate highway system (which was largely completed in the 1970s), and direct and indirect subsidization of the mass production of the automobile by government, have provided the means for easy commuting to outlying areas. Inadequate crime control efforts in the cities may have motivated people to seek to place ever-greater distances between themselves and the high crime rates that cities manifest. Federally-subsidized VA and FHA loan programs limited purchases to single-family dwellings and enabled the post-World War II construction boom of the single-family house in the suburbs during the 1950s and 1960s.[*13*] By the 1970s most suburbs adjacent to the central cities were almost fully developed so that developers were forced to look beyond the metropolitan land which could be profitably subdivided; almost half of all new housing built in the 1970s was located in rural areas.[*14*] Local land-use policies in the suburbs kept population density low and contributed to the early completion of development in metropolitan-area suburbs. Finally, court-ordered area-wide busing, school desegregation, and the loss of the cherished neighborhood school may have pushed white-flight beyond the suburbs to rural areas.[*15*] Persons who move to nonmetropolitan areas consistently cite the quality of schools as a major reason for their relocation.(16)

Geographic mobility generally and the public policies related to it and to the two migratory streams of the 1970s have generated a significant body of constitutional law and social science research, reflecting the extent and importance of these phenomena in American society. This material — including that on the related issue of population distribution — will be the concern of this chapter. The first question we will examine is the right of Americans to move from one state to another, after which we will consider the ability of state and local governments to regulate the number and types of people within their jurisdiction. The latter focus will be accompanied by a discussion of school desegregation. We will then investigate the ability of state and local governments to require public and private entities to prefer persons residing in their jurisdiction (especially those residing there for a period of time) in access to various items. This will be followed by a consideration of state policies preferring U.S. citizens over non-citizens. Such preferences have the purpose and/or effect of influencing migration patterns in the future or of capitalizing upon past migration patterns and the resulting distribution of population. Our focus here will include eligibility for such items as welfare, employment in the public and private sectors, and voting.

1. Migration Across State Lines

The first issue to be considered is the right of individuals to move from one state to another, temporarily or permanently, without restriction. The U.S. Supreme Court first dealt with the problem in 1968 when it faced a challenge to a State tax of one dollar for each person transported out of the state by commercial carrier.[17] The tax applied both to residents who were leaving the state and to transients who were simply crossing the state enroute from one point to another. In striking down the tax, reliance was not placed on a specific provision of the Constitution but, rather, on the intent of the document as a whole that there be a unified country under a national government. The Court recognized that a tax such as the one at issue, if it were made sufficiently large and/or if it were repeated by different states, could discourage or completely inhibit the movement of people. The result would be a burden on the ability of Americans to travel to and deal with the offices of their national government, whose capacity to function would be damaged accordingly. The Constitution did not intend, said the Court, for the federal government to be subservient to the States or for the status of national citizenship to be a mere adjunct to citizenship in a state. "For all the great purposes for which the Federal government was formed we are one people, with one common country. We are all citizens of the United States, and as members of the same community must have the right to pass and repass through every part of it without interruption, as freely as in our own States."[18]

The principal Supreme Court decision of recent vintage concerning internal migration was rendered in 1941 in *Edwards v. California*.[19] A state statute imposed criminal penalties for bringing, or assisting in bringing, an indigent person into the state with knowledge of his/her indigency. The statute was challenged by a California resident who had brought his brother-in-law to the state from Texas knowing that the latter was unemployed and dependent upon public welfare. Examining the statute under the Commerce Clause — which gives Congress rather than the states the authority to regulate that which is in or that which affects interstate commerce — the Supreme Court held the law invalid on the ground that states cannot erect barriers to the entry of persons who, for economic reasons, they consider undesirable. It should be noted that the statute did not impose penalties on the migrant personally but only on those others who, with knowledge of the migrant's indigency, were responsible for his/her presence in the state; it thus did not preclude nonresident indigents from entering the state if they could arrange private transportation without the assistance of others. That the Court ruled the law invalid even though it was not an absolute prohibition on immigration by indigents suggests the importance attached to freedom of geographic mobility. The high valuation of that freedom is further underscored by the historical context of the case. The State was attempting to minimize the problems it was facing from the severe economic depression of the 1930s. Even though the Supreme Court appeared to appreciate this,[20] it found the importance of national unity to outweigh the immediate advantages to the State. The Constitution, said the Court, was intended to impose a

> prohibition against attempts on the part of any single State to isolate itself from difficulties common to all of them by restraining the transportation of persons and property across its borders. It is frequently the case that a State might gain a momentary respite from the pressure of events by the simple expedient of shutting its gates to the outside world. But, in the words of Mr. Justice Cardozo: 'The Constitution was framed under the dominion of a political philosophy less parochial in range. It was framed upon the theory that the peoples of the several States must sink or swim together, and that in the long run prosperity and salvation are in union and not division'[21]

The concern with freedom of geographic mobility is also suggested implicitly by the very use of the Commerce Clause in *Edwards* to strike down the challenged statute, for the focus of the Clause is the nation as a whole. The Court could have found the statute to be a violation of the Fourteenth Amendment's guarantee of equal protection in singling out indigents and imposing criminal sanctions on those who assisted members of the class to move to the state. Had equal protection been employed, however, the Court would have had to focus on the *differences* between people created by the law, thereby precluding an exclusive emphasis on freedom of migration. The Commerce Clause permitted the Court to underscore the concern of the Constitution with national unity and the indispensable contribution of freedom of movement to that goal.

The public appears to be highly supportive of the principle manifested in *Edwards*. When a national sample was asked in 1976 whether "moving easily and freely from place to place" is important to our quality of life, almost nine in ten responded affirmatively.[22]

Building on the importance placed on freedom of movement by the American people and the judicial reflection of this value, a proposal was made in the 1970s for the government to relocate indigent urban residents who were willing to move to other areas where their quality of life and employment opportunities would be better. Under the plan, the federal government would assume the cost of relocation and of welfare payments until those relocated became self-supporting. The proposal was an extension of the right to freedom of movement in providing the financial means to move in search of a better life. It also aimed to insure the "labor force mobility" necessary for improving the national economy by moving the unemployed to jobs.[23] However, the public in the 1970s was less than totally supportive of governmentally-sponsored indigent mobility, and its support may have eroded in recent years. Table 4-3 indicates the level and trend of public approval for government relocation of the urban poor.

Table 4-3. Public Support in the U. S. for Government Relocation of the Urban Poor

Response	1974	1975	1977	1981
Favor	48%	47%	49%	44%
Oppose	44	46	42	48
No opinion	8	7	7	8

SOURCE: "Public divided on relocating urban poor" (1981). *The Gallup Report*, Report No. 188: 32-33.

By exhibiting overwhelming support for the right to freedom of movement but substantially less support for governmental financing of it for the indigent, the general public appears to be indicating that government should not inject itself into mobility decisions. Interstate mobility should be a matter of individual initiative rather than government intervention. This view is reflected in constitutional philosophy.

Another recent illustration of the societal value placed on freedom of movement and the use of the Commerce Clause to promote that freedom comes from a 1980 decision of the U.S. Court of Appeals for the Fifth Circuit (which covers Louisiana, Mississippi, and Texas), a decision that was affirmed without an opinion by the Supreme Court.[24] Pursuant to a state statute, an ordinance was adopted that required the registration with the police of persons who entered the county seeking employment as well as persons who were already employed there and who sought to change jobs. Unless a job applicant possessed an identification card showing (s)he had already registered or unless (s)he was a resident seeking his/her first position, every applicant was obligated by the ordinance to complete a form that included a photograph and fingerprints. Even though the applicant was not hired, the form was sent by the employer from whom it was completed to the police department, and a ten dollar fee was paid for each form by either the applicant or the employer.

The ordinance was found by the Court of Appeals to discriminate on its face against interstate commerce, because residents seeking their first job were not required to complete the form while nonresidents were. Given such facial discrimination, the question was whether there existed a sufficiently strong interest of the local goverment — which here was specified as the deterrence of criminal activity and the apprehension of persons who had committed crimes — and whether there were alternative measures that would advance the interest without discriminating against nonresidents. The court concluded that, although crime control is a legitimate concern of local government, there was inadequate evidence the measure at issue would accomplish this goal, and thus the ordinance could not stand. Moreover, even eliminating the facial discrimination against nonresidents and requiring everyone seeking employment in the county to complete the registration form, the court found the ordinance to be inconsistent with the Commerce Clause. The ten dollar fee was viewed as imposing an unacceptable hardship on migrant laborers, and alternative measures were thought to exist that would control crime without burdening interstate commerce.

An issue implicitly raised by the case is whether the Commerce Clause protects freedom of movement *within* a state. The ordinance imposed the same registration requirement on persons arriving from outside the state as it did on persons coming from within the state but another county. The fact that the Court of Appeals held the Commerce Clause applicable may indicate that intrastate movement that crosses a local government boundary is not to be distinguished from interstate movement; the protections of the Clause may apply to migration into the jurisdiction of *any* governmental body. On the other hand, the use of the Commerce Clause by the court may be interpreted simply as indicating that, since interstate movement was included in the coverage of the ordinance, the Clause applied. Even as to its application to intrastate movement exclusively, the court may have viewed migration as a national, and hence interstate, stream of which intrastate migration is an integral part. There is no certain answer at this time regarding whether the Commerce Clause applies to intrastate movement when interstate movement does not exist or is not affected,[25] but the question is potentially important. Situations may occur where a local government can deter in-migration by residents of its state if the Commerce Clause applies only when an interstate stream is involved.

The importance of freedom of geographic movement in constitutional philosophy is apparent, but one aspect of the opinion of the Supreme Court in *Edwards v. California* is worthy of note. While the members of the Court were uniformly of the view that the statute challenged there was invalid, a sharp division existed as to the appropriate constitutional basis for the decision. The five members of the majority relied on the Commerce Clause, but the remaining four members wrote concurring opinions to express their preference for the Privileges and Immunities Clause of the Fourteenth Amendment, which forbids States from abriding "the privileges or immunities of citizens of the United States." In the view of the four — who were reluctant to define the movement of human beings as "commerce" — Americans may travel from one state to another as a privilege conferred by their national citizenship.

It is not clear why the majority of the Court wanted to rely on the Commerce Clause. However, by doing so, it appears to have improved the likelihood that Congress can constitutionally regulate migration between the states. If the movement of people across state lines implicates interstate commerce, as the majority concluded, then Congress can control that movement under the authority it possesses from the Commerce Clause to regulate such commerce — authority which may include the prohibition of interstate movement.[26] Had travel across state lines been held a privilege of national citizenship, the opportunity for federal regulation would have been reduced. Even though the Fourteenth Amendment and its Privileges and Immunities Clause is a restriction on state governments only, a right to migrate to another state that emanates from national citizenship would have created more difficult constitutional problems for federal control of interstate movement. Such control may still be found to violate the guarantee of liberty provided individuals against federal government action under the Due Process Clause of the Fifth Amendment, but the probability and ease of finding a constitutional infringement would have been enhanced if movement across state lines was an attribute of United States citizenship.

The possibilities for federal control of interstate migration are suggested by an existing statute (known as the Travel Act) that permits the criminal prosecution of persons who cross a state line with the intent to commit or promote certain specified activities violating federal or state law.[27] The Act has been held to be a valid exercise of the authority granted Congress by the Commerce Clause and not inconsistent with other provisions of the Constitution.[28] In its present form, the Act bans conduct such as gambling, narcotics distribution, and arson — conduct that has been socially defined as inherently harmful.

The question, however, is what other activities may be included. Congress controls the channels of interstate commerce and can exclude from them persons who intentionally engage in conduct that is generally defined as a threat to social order. Those definitions can change. In 1917, the Supreme Court upheld a criminal conviction under a federal law for the transportation across a state line of a woman who was only the mistress of the defendant and not a prostitute.[29] In 1919, the Court upheld a federal law that prohibited crossing a state line with intoxicating liquor even though the liquor was for personal use, the state of destination did not prohibit such use, and only a small quantity (one quart) was involved.[30] While crossing a state line with a sexual partner who is not one's spouse or with alcoholic beverages for personal use probably does not violate public morals today, this only demonstates that social values change. With such change, unacceptable activity may not only become acceptable, but acceptable activity may become unacceptable. At some point in time, changed social and economic conditions may lead federal law to ban migration for conduct that is presently consistent with prevailing standards of morality.

While the Commerce Clause may empower Congress to restrict migration, it is not widely appreciated that the Clause also provides the authority for federal control over a wide range of activities relevant to interstate movement. Because of its authority over that which is within and that which affects interstate commerce, Congress is able to regulate everything involved with the movement of people and artifacts of theirs such as goods, services, and money. Under the Commerce Clause, federal statutes currently prohibit lenders from discriminating on the basis of sex and marital status in extending credit[31] and prohibit employers from discriminating on the basis of sex in the pay, hiring, and dismissal of employees.[32] The legislation reflects congruency in constitutional and statutory philosophy: "Employment decisions cannot be predicated on mere 'stereotyped' impressions about the characteristics of males and females. Myths and purely habitual assumptions about a woman's inability to perform certain kinds of work are no longer acceptable reasons for refusing to employ qualified individuals, or for paying them less."[33] Moreover, an employer cannot enforce policies that merely reflect the preferences of customers — e.g., for physically attractive females — unless the preferences are such that they will determine whether the employer can continue to operate.[35] Nor, it seems, can an employer enforce a policy simply because of its own preference if the result is that women are placed at a disadvantage. An employer is thus unable to discharge a female employee solely on the ground that she has had a child out of wedlock; because only females can become pregnant, a dismissal for pregnancy is based on gender, and because the marital status of a mother has no impact on job performance other than that caused by traditional definitions of sex roles, her dismissal for being unmarried is arbitrary and, hence, discriminatory.[36]

The Commerce Clause provides the constitutional basis for these statutory proscriptions because decisions in the realm of employment and credit have widespread consequences for Americans and their economic activity. The authority to regulate the national economy given Congress by the Clause is broad and, especially with regard to activities in the private sector, carries few limitations.

> [T]he power of Congress to regulate interstate commerce is plenary and extends to all such commerce be it great or small. The pertinent inquiry therefore is not how much commerce is involved but whether Congress could rationally conclude that the regulated activity affects interstate commerce.[37]

Statutory prohibitions of different treatment for men and women and their juridical interpretation in employment-related and commercial matters are closely related to changing public attitudes concerning the role of women in society. Generally, the public supports equal treatment for women in all respects of the marketplace; when statutes prohibiting sex discrimination in employment were enacted in the first half of the 1960s, there was overwhelming public endorsement of the principle of equal pay for equal work.[38] The legislation became the basis for the cases noted in the preceding paragraph when it was combined with the strong and rising support of the 1970s and early 1980s for equality in diverse facets of social life. As Table 4-4 shows, the proportion of Americans favoring "most efforts to strengthen and change women's status in society today"[39] increased from two out of five in 1970 to two out of three in 1981. The number of those who were undecided concerning the issue also declined sharply during this period.

Table 4-4. Percentages Favoring and Opposing Most Efforts to Change and Strengthen Women's Status in American Society Today

	1970	1971	1972	1975 Apr	1975 Dec	1977	1978	1979	1981
Favor	42%	49%	49%	59%	63%	64%	64%	65%	67%
Oppose	41%	36%	36%	28%	25%	27%	25%	28%	29%
Not Sure	17%	15%	16%	13%	12%	9%	11%	7%	4%

SOURCES: Louis Harris (1975). "Changing views on the role of women," *The Harris Survey*. Dec. 11: 1-2. Louis Harris (1979). "Women's movement gaining strength," *ABC News-Harris Survey*. March 8: 1-3. Louis Harris (1981). *The Harris Survey*. August 17: at 3.

By way of conclusion, it should be noted that there appears to be a relationship between three aspects of this section: The constitutional emphasis on freedom of migration for the individual; the role of the Commerce Clause in protecting that freedom and providing it with economic overtones; and, based on the federal control the Commerce Clause permits over that which affects the movement of people and their products, the statutory prohibition of sex discrimination in the economic arena. The three are interrelated, rather than independent, phenomena because of the operation of a common, underlying factor: The commitment of society to providing the individual with the opportunity to be upwardly mobile in its stratification system, especially the economic dimension of that system. The American ideal that individuals should be allowed to improve themselves and increase their material assets to the limit of their abilities[40] has affected the structure of society through, in part, constitutional interpretation and statutes grounded on constitutional provisions.

The constitutional concern with freedom of migration and the statutory suppression of gender-based barriers to advancement are thus manifestations of a more fundamental attribute of society. However, the ideal, in creating opportunities for socioeconomic and geographic mobility, has evidently operated through a number of societal phenomena concerned with economic progress. In addition to its direct impact on the interpretation of the Constitution and the enactment of statutes, the ideal facilitated the development of science in the nineteenth and twentieth centuries.[41] Significantly, the education of persons skilled in research — i.e., education at the doctorate level — began to increase economic productivity in the years just prior to *Edwards v. California*. Moreover, during the quarter-century preceding *Edwards*, secondary education rapidly expanded to support the American ideal and, in turn, enhance economic output.[42] *Edwards*, accordingly, was an integral part of American society and of the social forces that shaped it at the time.

2. Local Government Control of Population Numbers

Interstate and intrastate migration is related to efforts by local governments to control community population size, for such efforts affect the ability of people to cross state and county lines for the purpose of changing their residence. The decade of the 1970s witnessed intense interest in the control of population numbers by local governments. That interest was evidently promoted by changes in the occupational structure of the country which brought an increasing proportion of Americans into white-collar positions. It is particularly noteworthy that the rate of movement into such occupations in the decade preceding the interest was higher than in the decade before.[43] The changing occupational structure facilitated alterations in societal orientation, because white-collar positions create intellectual alertness and flexibility,[44] conditions increasing the likelihood that questions will be raised with regard to existing trends and that favorable attitudes toward the control of community growth will emerge.[45]

During the 1970s, Americans overwhelmingly supported the efforts of government to regulate land development and population distribution. However, while almost two-thirds of the public considered population distribution to be a serious problem,[46] more than half thought that their local governments had done no better than a fair job of regulating housing growth in their locality.[47] Given this general lack of confidence in the growth management efforts of local governments, almost two-thirds of the public thought the federal government should adopt population redistribution policies that would discourage growth in metropolitan areas and encourage growth in smaller places.[48]

The questions of federal government control of population distribution and of local control of population numbers are related to the more generalized question of national population growth. Population increase creates pressures for additional housing, jobs, and support services. These demands in turn raise the question of where to locate the additional residential, commercial and industrial development needed to accommodate additional population increments. Thus concern with population distribution is accompanied by a focus on the national growth that precedes and conditions localized developmental problems. Indeed, in the first half of the 1970s two-thirds of the public thought that population growth in the United States was a serious problem[49] and more than half thought it was more serious than population distribution. Further, three-fourths of the general public[50] and more than nine out of ten high school seniors thought that the current size of the American population should be smaller or at least no larger.[51]

Although public attention to the issue has waned in recent years, the debate continues on the need for and feasibility of community regulation of human numbers,[52] and this section will examine the constitutionality of action that local governments have taken in order to limit population size. As we will see, the means that have been used to control growth differed, as have the severity of the restrictions, and the differences were instrumental in accounting for the ability of the growth control policies to withstand court challenges to their constitutionality.

It is significant that the policies pursued by local governments were uniformly intended to limit population numbers by regulating the volume of in-migration and that the reduction of fertility was not their purpose. Indeed, some policies were adopted in order to promote housing characterized by considerable living space, a condition that fosters childbearing.[53] The failure of local governments to regulate fertility necessarily placed a limit on the effectiveness of their attempts to control growth. That failure, together with the constitutional restraints imposed on the ability of local governments to curtail migration, is probably responsible for the lack of success that growth containment policies have apparently experienced[54] and the discontent of the public with local growth management efforts. Let us turn to the constitutional restraints.

Perhaps the most direct and drastic approach employed to limit population numbers in a locality in the United States has been the adoption of a ceiling establishing a maximum number of dwelling units. Although the public generally approves of growth controls, there appears to be less-than-majority support for this kind of limitation; only two in ten continuously-married white women surveyed in 1970, and three in ten surveyed in 1975, believed that state and local governments have the right to limit population numbers directly.[55] The City of Boca Raton, Florida, pursued this approach in the mid-1970s by amending its charter to forbid the issuance of building permits for housing after a specified number of dwelling units had been reached.[56] A lengthy trial led to the conclusion that, without the ceiling, expected growth would not overburden the utility system and water supply and would not cause a deterioration in air quality and noise levels. Moreover, the growth that would occur without the ceiling would place the city in a better financial position by generating a larger surplus of revenue. The District Court of Appeal of Florida, an intermediate state appellate court, concluded that the ceiling therefore violated the constitutional guarantee to due process of law, a guarantee that permits restrictions on the right of landowners to use their property in an otherwise-acceptable manner only when government is acting to avert a clear threat to public welfare.

> The owner will not be required to sacrifice his rights absent a substantial need for restrictions in the interest of public health, morals, safety or welfare. If the zoning restriction exceeds the bounds of necessity for the public welfare,... [it] must be stricken as an unconstitutional invasion of property rights.[57]

It is important to note that the concept of a population ceiling *per se* was not declared invalid. The court left open the question whether a permanent limitation on population can be justified in some circumstances, because in the case before it, the evidence clearly indicated there was no need to curtail human numbers for environmental, resource, and financial reasons. Indeed, no court in the United States has faced an attempt to control population numbers where continued growth would exceed the absolute capacity of the environment and available resources. A ceiling has not been imposed where the limits to growth had unequivocally been reached and population increments could not be accomodated.

A second approach adopted by localities wanting to contain population numbers has been the denial of sewers to new housing. The highest courts of Colorado and New York have both invalidated such refusals.[58] It appears that sewers must be provided as long as the existing system will not be overloaded and that, where the capacity of the system will be exceeded, a delay in sewer connection will be tolerated only to the extent that the time is needed to expand the system. The public cannot impose on a particular landowner the entire economic burden of policies designed to protect the community permanently from population growth. Of course, the government may appropriate the property under its eminent domain powers, but only if it pays fair compensation for the land; if it is unwilling to do so, it must provide the facilities to accommodate growth.

> A police power regulation to be reasonable must be kept within the limits of necessity.... To justify interference with the beneficial enjoyment of property the municipality must establish that it has acted in response to dire necessity, that its action is reasonably calculated to alleviate or prevent the crisis condition, and that it is presently taking steps to rectify the problem.[59]

Local governments have employed a third approach to population control that has met with some, though limited, success in the courts. In this tactic, lots of substantial size have been required in the construction of housing on undeveloped land. In 1980, the U.S. Supreme Court approved the action of a California city that had restricted an area to a maximum of five single-family residences on five acres.[60] Since the landowner mounting the challenge to the restriction had never attempted to build on his property, the sole question facing the Court was whether just the enactment of a large lot requirement was unconstitutional. The mere existence of the requirement was in issue, not its application to a particular community or area within the community.

The action of the city was evaluated under the Fifth Amendment's prohibition against governmental appropriation of private property except when there has been payment of just compensation, and as to this constitutional provision, the Court concluded that it could find no violation. The large lot requirement was designed to maintain open space as the area developed and thus served a legitimate public purpose. The affected landowners received benefits from the requirement, because it permitted them to develop their land under a comprehensive plan that provided assurance to all concerned — including the purchasers of the homes ultimately built — that the area would possess a highly-valued attribute, namely, open space. Accordingly, a governmental taking of their property had not occurred. "The specific zoning regulations at issue are exercises of the city's police power to protect the residents of Tiburon from the ill-effects of urbanization. Such governmental purposes long have been recognized as legitimate."[61]

While the requirement of large lots for housing does not in principle involve an appropriation of private property by government, there have been specific situations where such a requirement has been found to be either a taking without just compensation (a violation of the Fifth Amendment) or an unreasonable restriction on the right of a landowner to the use of his/her property (a violation of the due process guarantee of the Fourteenth Amendment). The Supreme Court of Pennsylvania, for instance, ruled that a local government could not increase the lot size necessary for new houses from one acre to four.[62] The community was found to be facing population growth from the expanding metropolitan area of nearby Philadelphia, and the modification of its zoning ordinance appeared to be the result of a desire to deflect that expansion elsewhere. There was, however, no evidence that the greater population growth that would accompany smaller lot sizes would exceed the capacity of the sewage and road systems or of the water supply.

> The question posed is whether the township can stand in the way of the natural forces which send our growing population into hitherto undeveloped areas in search of a comfortable place to live. We have concluded not. A zoning ordinance whose primary purpose is to prevent the entrance of newcomers in order to avoid future burdens, economic and otherwise, upon the administration of public services and facilities can not be held valid.[63]

Moreover, the desire to preserve the rural character and aesthetic quality of the area was insufficient to justify the large lot requirement. The increased lot size did not create publicly-accessible open space but, rather, privately-owned preserves, and the requirement was thus not constitutionally permissible as an exercise of the police power to protect public interests.

> There is no doubt that many of the residents of this area are highly desirous of keeping it the way it is, preferring, quite naturally, to look out upon land in its natural state rather than on other homes. These desires, however, do not rise to the level of public welfare. This is purely a matter of private desire which zoning regulations may not be employed to effectuate.[64]

While a four-acre lot requirement was invalid, the original one-acre requirement was not at issue. The latter appears to have wide support, and the decision of the Supreme Court of Pennsylvania was thus not inconsistent with public values. In the 1970s three-fourths of Americans — regardless of whether they lived in city, suburb or rural area — chose single-family home ownership as their preferred type of housing.[65] The existence of space around the single-family house seems to be an important factor in this preference; in 1975 two-thirds of the public considered "a sizeable piece of land up to one acre" to be a very or fairly important determinant of the decision to purchase a house.[66]

The use of zoning to prevent population growth has also been challenged where communities have acted to exclude totally or curtail drastically the construction of multiple dwelling units. Local governmental restrictions on multi-family housing have been judicially negated despite the fact that they have substantial support among Americans. In the early 1970s, three-fourths of the public said they would like to see future development in their communities "take the form of single family" housing spread evenly throughout their area. Only about one in ten persons preferred apartment housing, even if it were clustered and interspersed with adequate open space. Only one in 17 preferred to see both kinds of development.[67] However, in spite of public preferences for single-family housing and for limitations on apartment construction, policies restricting multiple dwellings were invalidated by the supreme courts of New Jersey, New York, and Pennsylvania between 1975 and 1978.[68] The decisions reflect the American commitment to freedom of movement in their use of a criterion not previously emphasized — the need for housing in the community that emanates from population pressures in the region. In its zoning policies, a community that is in the process of developing must consider not only the needs of its own residents but the needs of residents of other areas as well. In spite of "the traditional view that zoning acts only upon the property lying within the zoning board's territorial limits, it must be recognized that zoning often has a substantial impact beyond the boundaries of the municipality."[69]

Just as the Commerce Clause unifies the United States, the police power that protects the welfare of the public demands that the larger geographic area in which a community finds itself be taken into account in local zoning decisions. Evidently this is true even though that area encompasses more than just the state in which the community is situated. The public welfare is a concept that has geographic breadth as well as substantive depth, and the police power does not permit the exclusion of needed high-density housing from a developing locality.

A community that is not interfering with population growth, except incidentally to the extent needed to protect important values, has more latitude for its action, because it is not directly threatening the societal concern with freedom of movement. A constitutional violation occurs when there is a governmental purpose to avoid substantial increments in human numbers in situations where those increments can be accommodated without a serious reduction in the existing standard of living. Action that is designed to promote the welfare of residents and that is not intended to avert significant increases in population numbers appears to be constitutionally sound. In such a situation, there is no violation of the Constitution when a community limits the number of units in a condominium project to a level far below the maximum the developer believes can be built and sold.[70] The U.S. Court of Appeals for the Third Circuit (which covers Delaware, New Jersey, and Pennsylvania) concluded that there was no infringement here of the due process guarantee of the Fourteenth Amendment, because local government may act reasonably — as it was found to have done — to control population density, at least where the community is not a developing one into which people from the region need to move. Quality of life, the court noted, is very much affected by the number of people in an area, and when it is seriously jeopardized and other overriding considerations are not present, government can take appropriate measures that are reasonable in nature.

> The police power is not confined to elimination of filth, stench, and unhealthy places. It is ample to lay out zones where family values, youth values, and the blessings of quiet seclusion and clean air make the area a sanctuary for people.[71]

In addition, the court concluded that the limitation on development did not infringe the Fifth Amendment prohibition against governmental appropriation of private property except when fair compensation is paid. There was no taking of property, because the limitation was applicable throughout the zone in which the land of the challenger was located, it would to some extent enhance the price of the smaller number of units built, and its effect in diminishing land value (about one-third here) was of insufficient magnitude.

A decision of the highest state court of Maryland provides another, and perhaps more forceful, illustration of the ability of local government to curtail in-migration when it is not attempting to isolate the community. In this case, a County Commission restricted the number of bedrooms that would be permitted in new apartment buildings in order to alleviate pressures on the public school system; a maximum of ten per cent of all units in a proposed project could have three or more bedrooms and a maximum of 40 per cent could have two bedrooms.[72] The restriction was challenged on two grounds: That it did not promote the general welfare and thus constituted an unreasonable restraint on private property in violation of the guarantee of due process; and that it increased the difficulty faced by large families in locating appropriate housing and thus created a class in violation of the guarantee of equal protection. Rejecting both arguments and upholding the restriction, the court noted that the population of the county had doubled in the preceding decade, that the problems accompanying such rapid growth made the control of density legitimate, and that the means adopted by the County Commission were reasonable in achieving this end.

In communities that are well-developed, then, local government can act to dampen population growth even though it cannot act to impede growth seriously or avoid it totally. When confronted by population increments that are jeopardizing essential public services and the standard of living, local government can adopt measures that slow the increase in human numbers to a manageable level. Those measures, if reasonable, may determine the number of dwellings in a given amount of space or their internal structure. In the interest of population limitation, there may even be a limit on the number of unrelated persons who live together,[73] though the living arrangements of family members may not be regulated except insofar as those arrangements may be affected by generally-applicable density controls.[74]

Let us, finally, examine policies that have been implemented in order to establish a pre-determined rate of growth for a substantial period of time. Under this approach, the construction of new housing has been controlled and the level of construction permitted has been set below that which would have otherwise occurred, but there has been no attempt to permit only negligible increases in population. Two court cases are prominent here, and in both, the policies were approved. In the first, the U.S. Court of Appeals for the Ninth Circuit (which covers Alaska, Arizona, California, Hawaii, Idaho, Montana, Nevada, Oregon, and Washington) upheld a city regulation that restricted the annual increase in housing to 500 dwelling units in projects in which at least five units were to be built. No restriction, however, was placed on the construction of single-family homes or multiple dwellings that had fewer than five units.[75] The policy was found to allow a six per cent increase each year in the number of dwelling units in the city, and even though it might exclude a substantial number of people who would have moved to the area, the court concluded that the restriction was justified by the public interest in preserving low population density and in experiencing growth that was predictable and planned.

The second case involving a policy of slow growth arose when a New York municipality imposed controls on the development of subdivisions.[76] Building permits for subdivisions were to be issued as public facilities (e.g., sewers, parks, schools, and roads) became adequate. The municipality undertook to provide the needed facilities and guaranteed that, at the end of 18 years, permits would be issued to any developer not having yet obtained one. Moreover, if the facilities were not adequate when a developer wished to proceed, a building permit could be obtained if the developer provided the facilities at his/her own expense. The highest state court approved the controls on the ground there was a strong public interest in planned growth that justified the restraints on the use of private property. Even though the restraints might entail a substantial delay, the municipality had a constitutionally viable policy because it was not seeking

> to freeze population at present levels but to maximize growth by the efficient use of land, and in so doing testify to this community's continuing role in population assimilation. In sum, Ramapo asks not that it be left alone, but only that it be allowed to prevent the kind of deterioration that has transformed well-ordered and thriving residential communities into blighted ghettos with attendant hazards to health, security and social stability....[77]

Significantly, the social-economic deterioration of communities appears to be a consequence of growth in their populations.[78] Numerical increase is generally followed by social and economic decline. That is, moreover, no reason at present to expect that pressures to enlarge communities will abate. Population growth in the United States as a whole remains at a substantial level from natural increase and immigration. Of more immediate impact, there is appreciable net migration to suburban and nonmetropolitan areas, and migrants entering these areas are characterized by larger families than migrants leaving them.[79] The question thus arises whether constitutional philosophy, in seriously restraining efforts to limit population numbers in communities, is dysfunctional for the society in which it exists and as such is likely to be abandoned.

A doctrine used by society that is in some ways dysfunctional is unlikely to be deeply embedded in the social fabric — as is constitutional philosophy regarding community efforts to control growth — unless it provides an offsetting and important benefit. A doctrine producing some negative effects that does not possess significant social utility will find it difficult to gain and retain appreciable influence. What is the utility of the constitutional philosophy here? The answer appears to lie in the American stratification system. By preserving the opportunity of the individual to move, the philosophy makes accessible areas of higher economic status and more desired housing (a topic we will consider in more depth shortly).[80] It thus supports the societal belief that distinctions in wealth can be overcome by skill and diligence, a belief that in the United States appears to be essential to preserving social peace in the midst of a class structure. Constitutional philosophy, in maintaining access to communities, improves the credibility of the belief that personal advancement is possible and that differences in wealth reflect differences in ability and perseverance. The belief reduces social tensions and the likelihood of class-based conflict.

> [E]very society, in the face of its particular historical contingencies, provides a rationale, myth or belief that enables its members to cope with their position in the stratification system. Such a rationale invites people to accept and condone existing inequality as generally just and reasonable.[81]

3. Local Government and Population Composition

Local governments have acted to regulate not only the *number* of people in a community but also the *types* of people. In particular, the zoning power has been used in attempts to restrict the entry of low-income and minority groups. That power, however, has achieved these goals primarily in suburban locations, where zoning has tended to increase segregation on the basis of income and, to a lesser extent, on the basis of race.[82] The differential impact of zoning on segregation by income and by race is consistent with constitutional philosophy regarding the ability of government to discriminate on these two criteria. That philosophy, which is more tolerant of wealth-based than of race-based discrimination, evidently reflects the degree of importance of each type of discrimination to the American stratification system.[83]

The leading decision of the U.S. Supreme Court relevant to zoning practices of a discriminatory nature is *Village of Arlington Heights v. Metropolitan Housing Development Corporation*, a decision rendered in 1977.[84] The case involved a Chicago suburb dominated by detached single-family homes that were occupied almost exclusively by Caucasians. The litigation arose when the municipal government refused to rezone a parcel of land to permit low- and moderate-income multiple-family housing that was expected to be racially integrated. No violation of the guarantee of equal protection was found, however, given that the consistent policy of the municipality had been to permit only single-family homes to be constructed for residential dwellings in the area where the parcel was located.

In its opinion, the Supreme Court was careful to emphasize that the critical element in an equal protection violation is the presence of an improper governmental *purpose*. Government action that has different *effects* between groups does not create a constitutional problem, though it may be used as evidence in determining purpose.

> [O]fficial action will not be held unconstitutional solely because it results in a racially disproportionate impact is not irrelevant, but it is not the sole touchstone of an invidious racial discrimination. Proof of racially discriminatory intent or purpose is required to show a violation of the Equal Protection Clause.[85]

In zoning that hampers members of minority groups, the question is whether government has been motivated by an invidious — i.e., injurious — purpose directed toward these groups. In *Village of Arlington Heights*, the Court could find no such purpose because of its conclusion that the municipality had acted to preserve the aesthetic character of the neighborhood and the quality of life of its residents. Racial considerations were not present, and the effect on minority racial groups was thus constitutionally unimportant.

It is relevant to point out here the nature of the remedial action that can be judicially ordered when there has been discrimination by a governmental entity. When that entity is an arm of the federal government — which is extensively involved in providing funds for housing[86] — courts may order housing subject to its control to be developed outside the geographic area in which the constitutional violation occurred. A federal agency operates throughout a region, and its conduct under the remedial order can be so molded that there will be no interference with local governmental units that are outside the area of, and that were not inplicated in the discrimination. Accordingly, even though a federal agency racially discriminated only within a city in selecting sites for public housing, the Supreme Court in *Hills v. Gautreaux* concluded that the agency could be required to use the entire metropolitan area to rectify the resulting segregation. Social policy requires that "in the event of a constitutional violation all reasonable methods be available to formulate an effective remedy and that every effort should be made by a federal court to employ those methods to achieve the greatest possible degree of relief, taking into account the practicalities of the situation."[87]

The existence of an invidious purpose is, however, only the first step in the inquiry as to whether there is a violation of the equal protection guarantee; its presence does not automatically create a constitutional infringement. An invidious purpose leads to the assessment of the governmental action according to the appropriate constitutional standard. The standard to be used, in turn, depends upon the object of the discrimination.

When government acts to deter persons of low income from moving into an area, it creates a classification based on wealth. Such a classification is constitutionally suspect if indigents are totally unable to pay for a governmentally-controlled benefit *and* are completely deprived of the opportunity to secure the benefit. A classification based on race — i.e., a classification emanating from a racially-discriminatory invidious purpose — is, however, inherently suspect. If a classification is deemed suspect, the equal protection guarantee is satisfied only if government can demonstrate that its action furthers a compelling public interest by the narrowest possible means. If the classification is not suspect, the action of government need just be reasonably related to a legitimate public interest. The former test, being more severe than the latter, is more likely to result in the invalidation of the challenged action.

To illustrate, a California municipality pursued a zoning policy that mandated a minimum of one acre of land for a residential lot and a maximum of one dwelling unit on a lot. The policy was challenged in the mid-1970s by a developer who planned low-income multiple-family housing on a tract of land. The U.S. Court of Appeals for the Ninth Circuit concluded that, since adequate low-income housing was available elsewhere in the county, the zoning policy did not completely deprive indigents of an opportunity to obtain suitable housing and hence did not create a suspect class. Using the less stringent test, the court upheld the policy on the ground that it was rationally related to the legitimate interest of the municipality in preserving its rural environment.[88]

While the exclusion of low-income housing does not create a suspect class except under limited conditions, the exclusion of such housing when motivated by racial bias does. Courts, however, seem unwilling to assume that hostility to low-income housing *per se* constitutes hostility based on race. Persons of low income are more likely to be Black (or of Spanish origin) than to be Caucasian,[89] but the statistical relationship between income and race is insufficient to prove a racial motivation in the context of zoning for housing. Evidence of a more direct nature is required for the conclusion that racial considerations lay behind opposition to low-income housing. As an example of the evidence required, opposition by the City of Philadelphia to a low-income public housing project was found to have an invidious racial purpose when the opposition stemmed from racially-biased statements, and the City attempted to terminate the project knowing that minority racial groups would disproportionately suffer from termination.[90] However, even if evidence does not exist of personal bias on the part of municipal officials, their action will be deemed to have a racial purpose if it is a response to and implements community hostility that is racially motivated.[91]

In the 1960s and 1970s, the public appeared to be characterized by definite attitudes toward residential segregation and the criteria for it. Americans seemed generally supportive of segregation by socioeconomic status throughout the period,[92] and the acceptance by the Supreme Court in 1977 of the exclusion of multi-family housing in *Arlington Heights* reflects this consensus. Segregation based on race also attracted considerable support, but that support declined significantly during the period. Approximately four out of ten Whites reported in the mid-1960s that they would be inclined to change their residence if Blacks moved in "next door," but by the late 1970s only one in ten gave this response. If Blacks "came to live in great numbers" in their neighborhood, seven out of ten Whites in the mid-1960s indicated that they would be tempted to move, but by the late 1970s only half reported they would be so inclined.[93] The lessened resistance to racial integration was evidently manifested in the 1976 decision of the Court in *Hills v. Gautreaux* to permit metropolitan-wide remedies to government-caused residential segregation. Indeed, in the four-year period preceding the decision, the proportion of Whites believing they did not have a right to exclude Blacks from their neighborhood was steady at six out of ten,[94] suggesting a stable and solid foundation for the position taken by the Court.

In the 1960s and 1970s, then, approval of segregation in housing was strong and constant with regard to socioeconomic status but not with regard to race. This indicates that socioeconomic status is a more important and deeply-embedded dimension of the structure of society than is race. Constitutional philosophy suggests this as well. In determining the constitutionality of government action, the exclusion of housing from a community on the basis of income and wealth is normally subject only to the least stringent test, while such an exclusion that is racially motivated will be evaluated by the most stringent standard.

4. School Desegregation

The exclusion of minority racial groups from housing in communities is related to racial segregation in the public schools, for the principle of the neighborhood school has meant that segregation in housing is carried over into the school system. The measures taken to eliminate segregated schools have created an issue of unusual social divisiveness; indeed, only one other issue in constitutional law — abortion — has attracted a comparable level of attention in the last half of the twentieth century.

Segregation in the public schools emerged as a major issue at mid-century with the 1954 decision of the U.S. Supreme Court in *Brown v. Board of Education*.[95] Segregation in public facilities had been legally acceptable since the 1890s when the Supreme Court ruled that a state law requiring separate train coaches for Blacks and Whites did not violate the Equal Protection Clause of the Fourteenth Amendment.[96] This "separate but equal" doctrine provided the constitutional foundation for state legislation which required racially-segregated schools. Such *de jure* school systems were the norm in the South during the first half of the twentieth century.[97]

The issue of racial segregation in American life rose to prominence in the public forum immediately following World War II. In part, this can be attributed to American opposition to Nazi racism, opposition that came to contrast sharply with racial segregation at home.[98] However, another force also apparently operated to make segregation a salient issue. The migration of large numbers of Blacks from the South rapidly increased the proportion of Blacks in central city populations in the North and West starting in the early 1940s.[99] Southern Blacks were characterized by lower educational levels than those born and reared in the North and West, and they raised the level of residential segregation by race.[100] The probable result within the black communities and subculture of urban areas outside the South [101] was enhanced pressure to improve the opportunities of Blacks for education and social-economic mobility. Given the impetus that urban areas give to concepts and conduct inconsistent with established patterns,[102] a challenge to school segregation was predictable.

The political discussion of discrimination and segregation in the immediate post-war period led pollsters to test public sentiment concerning these issues. Desegregation of schools had not yet attracted serious national attention, because it was not directly related to the wartime context of the civil rights of black adults. Since discrimination in hiring and integration of interstate travel are closely related to desegregation of schools, public attitudes toward these two issues will be examined as indicators of desegregation attitudes generally prior to the *Brown* decision.

In 1945 and 1946, the public was almost equally divided over state legislation requiring employers to hire persons regardless of race or color: Two out of five favored the legislation, while the same number opposed it.[103] By 1947, public sentiment for equal employment opportunity for Blacks had grown slightly. Half the general public believed that Blacks should have an equal chance at "every kind of job."[104]

Building on the visibility of the minority rights issue, President Harry Truman in 1948 proposed a civil rights package as a part of his presidential election campaign that included legislation to prohibit discrimination in hiring.[105] Survey questions on this issue were thus asked prior to and after the election, as polls attempted to assess degrees of commitment to a federal program which would require employers to provide equal employment opportunity. Table 4-5 presents the results.

The data in Table 4-5 indicate that about four out of ten persons favored some sort of federal legislation in this area in 1948 and 1949. However, an increase in approval was subsequently registered and about half did so in 1950. Support in the South, however, was much less, with only one in five approving such legislation. Still, even Southerners exhibited increasing support for equal employment legislation in the late 1940s.

Public attitudes were also sampled during this period with regard to the integration of buses and trains that cross state lines. Attitudes were studied in apparent response to the Supreme Court decision in 1946 that state laws requiring racial separation on such buses and trains disrupt interstate travel and violate the Commerce Clause.[106] Table 4-6 indicates that the desegregation of interstate carriers received substantial endorsement in 1948 and 1949 in the nation at large and majority support outside the South. Moreover, resistance to desegregation appears to have declined, as evidenced by a drop in the proportion favoring segregation and a rise in the proportion holding no opinion.

While civil rights for Blacks in employment and travel attracted considerable national attention during the late 1940s, the issue of school desegregation was far less visible. A focus on education came first from court action in the South at the college level. Civil rights activists felt that the issue of segregation in public schools was best broached in higher education, especially graduate programs, rather than at the secondary or elementary level. Several considerations were the basis for this strategy. Discrepancies between black and white graduate programs were great, and in many cases equivalent black programs were nonexistent. It was also felt that southerners would be more receptive to the integration of adults than to that of their children.[107] Finally, after World War II, the GI Bill provided black as well as white veterans with the opportunity to attend college so that there were sufficient potential litigants.[108] Thus the first challenges to segregation in educational facilities came when Blacks were ordered admitted to graduate programs in state universities in Missouri in 1938,[109] and in Oklahoma and Texas in the post-War period,8110] because there were no separate but equal programs for them in black colleges.

Table 4-5. Public Approval of Federal Equal Employment Legislation during the Post-War Period in the United States

Question: How far do you, yourself, think the Federal Government should go in requiring employers to hire people without regard to race, religion, color, or nationality?

Response	NATIONAL				SOUTH ONLY	
	1948 March	1948 Nov.	1949	1950	1948	1949
All the way	32%	34%	34%	34%	9%	15%
Depends on type of work or part of the way	7%	8%	5%	14%	3%	5%
Sub-total	39%	42%	39%	48%	12%	20%
Should leave matter to the states	2%	-	2%	-	2%	2%
Should do nothing	45%	44%	45%	41%	68%	64%
No opinion	14%	14%	14%	11%	18%	14%
Total	100%	100%	100%	100%	100%	100%

SOURCES: George H. Gallup (1972). *The Gallup Poll, Public Opinion: 1935-1971*, v. 1, *1935-1948*, v. 2, *1949-1958*. New York: Random House, at 747-8, 782-3, 810. Mildred Strunk (1950). "The quarter's polls," *Public Opinion Quarterly*, 14 (Spring): 174-192. Data from this article are reprinted by copyright 1950 by The Trustees of Columbia University.

Table 4-6. Public Support for Desegregation of Travel in the Post-War Period in the United States

Question: Do you think Negroes should or should not be required to occupy a separate part of a train or bus when traveling from one state to another?

Response	NATIONAL			OUTSIDE SOUTH		SOUTH	
	1948 March	1948 Nov.	1949	1948	1949	1948	1949
Should	42%	43%	38%	36%	32%	84%	79%
Should not	49%	49%	50%	54%	55%	12%	14%
No opinion	9%	8%	12%	10%	13%	4%	7%
Total	100%	100%	100%	100%	100%	100%	100%

SOURCES: George H. Gallup (1972). *The Gallup Poll, Public Opinion: 1935-1971*, v. 1, *1935-1948*, v. 2, *1949-1958*. New York: Random House, at 747-8, 782-3, and 810.

Following these rulings, a 1952 survey of Southern college students at two Texas universities, one black and one white, found immediate acceptance of integration of graduate programs. Only one in five opposed such integration.[111]

It should be noted that the initial decisions of the Supreme Court did not question the separate but equal doctrine itself nor did they apply to lower levels of education. Blacks could only be admitted to white universities when black colleges were undeniably unequal. Discrepancies in lower-level educational programs were not as apparent or as readily proved. Consequently, school desegregation did not become a nationwide issue nor did pollsters test national opinion on it extensively until the Court rendered its decision in *Brown v. Board of Education*

Brown nonetheless did not occur in a vacuum. It was undertaken and decided in the context of the university cases and of the public support for desegregation generally which characterized post-War ideology. With regard to the desegregation of primary and secondary schools, there is some evidence of appreciable and growing approval: In 1950, four out of ten persons evidenced support of integrated schools, an increase from three out of ten in the early 1940s.[112] Thus, *Brown v. Board of Education* was accepted for argument before the Supreme Court in 1952 and decided in 1954, a time when the national commitment to segregation in primary and secondary schools had seriously eroded.

In *Brown*, the Court tackled the State-required racial separation in primary and secondary school systems of the South, an issue affecting far greater numbers of Americans than university-level controversies. The Court held that segregated schools are unconstitutional even when they do not differ in terms of physical facilities and other objective measures (e.g., the educational credentials of the faculty). Racially-segregated schools create psychological problems for children of minority races and affect their intellectual development, with the result that "separate educational facilities are inherently unequal."[113]

The far-reaching consequences of the *Brown* case on American education generated intense public interest in school desegregation. Thus, in the years following the decision, levels of public approval were continually tapped by the polls. Table 4-7 presents data concerning level of approval for the principle of desegregation established by the decision.

Table 4-7. Public Acceptance of the *Brown* Decision (United States)

Question: The United States Supreme Court has rule that racial segregation in the public schools is illegal. This means that all children, no matter what their race, must be allowed to go to the same schools. Do you approve or disapprove of this decision?

NATIONAL

	1954	1955 April	1955 Nov.	1956	1957 April	1957 July	1957 Sept.	1959	1961
Approve	54%	56%	59%	63%	62%	58%	59%	57%	62%
Disapprove	41%	38%	37%	31%	32%	36%	35%	35%	33%
No opinion	5%	6%	4%	6%	6%	6%	6%	6%	5%
	100%	100%	100%	100%	100%	100%	100%	100%	100%

SOUTH ONLY

	1954	1955	1956	1957 April	1957 Sept.	1959	1961
Approve	24%	20%	27%	27%	23%	22%	24%
disapprove	71%	73%	67%	67%	72%	71%	69%
No opinion	5%	7%	6%	6%	5%	7%	7%
	100%	100%	100%	100%	100%	100%	100%

SOURCES: George H. Gallup (1972). *The Gallup Poll, Public Opinion: 1935-1971.* New York: Random House. V. 2, *1949-1958*, at 1249, 1332-3, 1401, 1420, 1465, 1487, 1518. V. 3, *1959-1971*, at 1616, 1723.

The data suggest that immediately following the *Brown* decision more than half the general public approved of the Court's action, while only one-fourth of southerners did so. In the seven-year period thereafter, six out of ten persons nationally gave their approval. In the South, support held steady at about one out of four or five persons. Outside the South, between seven and eight persons in ten approved of the *Brown* principle.[114]

There appears to have been a rallying effect for the Supreme Court in support of its decision in *Brown* as there was for its decision on abortion in 1973, but the effect was less noticeable in the former case. Support for the principle of desegregation in schools did not substantially increase nationwide or in the South until well into the 1960s when the civil rights movement was in full swing.[115] This is exemplified by the attitudes of white parents with school-age children who were asked to indicate whether they would object to sending their children to schools in which few, half, and more than half of the students were Black. Table 4-8 shows that, outside the South, objections to schools with a few Blacks fell in the late 1950s and then held steady; that objections to schools equally divided racially declined in the mid- to late-1960s; and that objections to predominantly Black schools fluctuated considerably over time.

In the South, however, greater changes occurred. In the late 1950s, seven out of ten White parents in the region expressed objections to sending their children to schools characterized by even token integration, but the first half of the 1960s witnessed a dramatic decline in such objections and resistance continued to fall steadily until 1980. A decline is also seen in objections to schools in which half of the children are Black; schools that are equally-divided racially experienced an initial drop in hostility in the first part of the 1960s, but a more rapid drop in the last part, with the decline continuing at a reduced pace in subsequent years. For schools with prominent numbers of White students, then, the attitudes of southerners regarding integration softened measurably during the 1960s, with major change occurring first with regard to schools characterized by minimal integration and later with regard to schools characterized by equal numbers of Blacks and Whites. The relative speed of the decline in the 1960s is significant in view of the Supreme Court cases discussed below that promoted school integration in the South during the decade. The attitudinal

Table 4-8. Support of Levels of School Integration Among White Parents of School-Age Children (United States)

OUTSIDE SOUTH

Question: Would you, yourself, have any objection to sending your children to a school where a few of the children are colored/Black?

	1954	1958	1095	1965	1966	1969	1970	1973	1975	1978*	1980
Would object	-	13%	7%	7%	6%	7%	6%	6%	3%	5%	5%
Would not object	-	86%	92%	91%	93%	93%	-	94%	-	92%	-
No opinion	-	1%	1%	2%	1%	-	-	-	-	3%	-

Question: .... where half the children are colored/Black?

	1954	1958	1095	1965	1966	1969	1970	1973	1975	1978*	1980
Would object	-	39%	34%	28%	32%	28%	24%	27%	24%	25%	22%
Would not object	-	56%	63%	65%	64%	69%	-	73%	-	69%	-
No opinion	-	5%	3%	7%	4%	3%	-	-	-	7%	-

Question: ... where more than half of the children are colored/Black?

	1954	1958	1095	1965	1966	1969	1970	1973	1975	1978*	1980
Would object	**54%	58%	58%	52%	60%	54%	51%	63%	47%	41%	51%
Would not object	**41%	36%	35%	37%	32%	39%	-	37%	-	53%	-
No opinion	5%	6%	7%	11%	8%	7%	-	-	-	6%	-

* Figures are for all Whites nationwide including South.
** In 1954, the question was "Would you object to having your children attend a school where the majority of pupils are Negro?"

Table 4-8 (Continued). Part II: Support of Levels of School Integration Among White Parents of School-Age Children (United States)

SOUTH ONLY

Question: Would you, yourself, have any objection to sending your children to a school where a few of the children are colored/Black?

	1954	1959	1965	1966	1969	1970	1973	1975	1978	1980
Would object	72%	72%	37%	24%	21%	16%	16%	15%	7%	5%
Would not object	26%	25%	62%	74%	78%	-	84%	-	88%	-
No opinion	2%	3%	1%	2%	1%	-	-	-	5%	-

Question: ... where half the children are colored/Black?

	1954	1959	1965	1966	1969	1970	1973	1975	1978	1980
Would object	81%	83%	68%	49%	46%	43%	36%	38%	28%	27%
Would not object	15%	12%	27%	44%	47%	-	64%	-	67%	-
No opinion	4%	5%	5%	7%	7%	-	-	-	5%	-

Question: ... where more than half of the children are colored/Black?

	1954	1959	1965	1966	1969	1970	1973	1975	1978	1980
Would object	84%	86%	78%	62%	64%	69%	69%	61%	49%	66%
Would not object	11%	8%	16%	27%	26%	-	31%	-	45%	-
No opinion	5%	6%	6%	11%	10%	-	-	-	6%	-

SOURCES: George H. Gallup (1972). *The Gallup Poll, Public Opinion, 1935-1971.* New York: Random House. V. 2, *1949-1958,* at 1251, 1569; v. 3, *1959-1971,* at 1598, 1940-1, 2010, 2211.

George H. Gallup (1978). *The Gallup Poll, Public Opinion, 1972-1977.* Wilmington, DE.: Scholarly Resources, at 179.
George H. Gallup (1979). *The Gallup Poll, Public Opinion, 1978.* Wilmington, DE.: Scholarly Resources, at 216.
"Whites and Blacks in sharp disagreement on busing/white parents' acceptance of integrated schools has grown since 1958" (1981). *The Gallup Report,* Report No. 185: 28-30.

change among southerners at this time was presumably both a facilitator and reflection of these decision.

The Court found it necessary to continue dealing with school segregation, because the means of accomplishing integration had generated serious resistance and considerable litigation in the years following *Brown*. The Court had explicitly recognized that there may be a legitimate need to dismantle a segregated school system gradually over time rather than immediately, a need that may arise from limitations in such resources as physical plant, personnel, and transportation facilities. However, it insisted "that delay in any guise in order to deny the constitutional rights of Negro children could not be countenanced, and that only a prompt start, diligently and earnestly pursued, to eliminate racial segregation from the public schools could constitute good faith compliance" with constitutional dictates.[116] On the other hand, the public for the most part preferred gradual to immediate integration throughout the 1950s and 1960s. Only between one and two in ten persons in both decades thought that integration should be accomplished immediately or that it was not going fast enough.[117] Significantly, research to date suggests that judicially-approved programs have been ineffective in eliminating segregation in schools and housing.[118]

Our examination of Supreme Court cases dealing with school integration in the South in the 1960s — a review which is illustrative rather than exhaustive — begins with a 1964 decision. The case involved a county that had closed all of its public schools rather than integrate them and that had developed private schools to educate school-age children. The closing of the public schools was accompanied by state and county enactments of tuition grant programs for children attending private nonsectarian schools — which grants provided the principal source of revenue for the schools — and by a county ordinance authorizing payments made to schools to be applied as a credit on property taxes that could reduce such taxes as much as 25 per cent. While every other county in the state continued its public schools, the Court assumed that a county was not required to do so. Nevertheless, an infringement of the equal protection guarantee was found in the situation. The State was treating children in the county in question in a different manner than it treated those in other counties, for the former were required to attend racially-segregated schools while the latter were not. A State, through its political subdivisions, need not be characterized by uniformity throughout its jurisdiction, but measures such as those taken in the county here to maintain segregated schools were not acceptable. "Whatever nonracial grounds might support a state's allowing a county to abandon public schools, the object must be a constitutional one, and grounds of race and opposition to desegregation do not qualify as constitutional."[119]

In 1968, a different type of situation confronted the Court. A school board in a county having no residential segregation had adopted a "freedom of choice" plan three years earlier for integrating its racially-segregated school system. The plan allowed each student to choose the school that (s)he would attend. However, in the three years the plan had been in operation, the schools remained segregated, leading the Court to hold that the school board was under a constitutional duty to implement an effective desegregation program. Delegation of the choice of school to children and their parents was unacceptable, since the evidence indicated the approach did not work. Freedom of choice programs, however, were not declared unconstitutional *per se*. The question was whether there was a factual basis for believing that such an approach was reasonably likely to promote integration given the alternatives available.

> Where it offers real promise of aiding a desegregation program to effectuate conversion of a state-imposed dual system to a unitary, nonracial system there might be no objection to allowing such a device to prove itself in operation. On the other hand, if there are reasonably available other ways... promising speedier and more effective conversion to a unitary, nonracial school system, 'freedom of choice' must be held unacceptable.[120]

Since school integration did not proceed at a satisfactory rate during the 1960s, busing was devised as a way to achieve racial balance. Busing first received Supreme Court approval in 1971 [121] and since then has been an emotionally-laden topic. Prior to the Court ruling, only about one in ten persons favored busing as a means to achieve desegregation, as shown in Table 4-9, and in the years following the ruling, only about two in ten were favorable. However, since the higher level of favorable attitudes appears shortly after the Court's approval of the approach in April 1971, the public apparently exhibited a rallying effect of a rather durable nature.

Table 4-9. Support and Opposition to Busing (United States)

Question: Do you favor or oppose busing?

	1970	1971 Aug.	1971 Oct.	1972	1974	1975	1976	1977	1978	1980	1982
Favor	11%	19%	18%	20%	18%	20%	14%	16%	21%	22%	28%
Oppose	86%	73%	76%	80%	72%	74%	81%	84%	79%	72%	72%
Not sure/ Don't know	3%	8%	6%	-	10%	6%	5%	-	-	6%	-
	100%	100%	100%	100%	100%	100%	100%	100%	100%	100%	100%

SOURCES: George H. Gallup (1972). *The Gallup Poll. Public Opinion, 1935-1971,* v. 3, *1959-1971.* New York: Random House, at 2243-4, 2323.
Louis Harris (1975). "Desegregation? Yes. Busing? No." *The Harris Survey.* Oct. 2: 2.
Louis Harris (1976). "Public willing to obey courts on busing," *The Harris Survey.* July 8: 1.
"Surveys chart changes in racial attitudes since '63 'March on Washington'" (1978). *The Gallup Opinion Index,* Report No. 160: 21-29.
"During 1950s Gallup surveys show widening approval of Supreme Court decision barring segregated schools/busing controversy dominates 1970s, with 7 in 10 opposed" (1981). *The Gallup Report,* Report No. 185: 25-27.
"Whites and Blacks in sharp disagreement on busing/white parents' acceptance of integrated schools has grown since 1958" (1981). *The Gallup Report,* Report No. 185: 28-30.
George H. Gallup (1982). *The Gallup Poll. Public Opinion 1981.* Wilmington, DE.: Scholarly Resources, at 21.
"Public opinion referendum" (1982). *The Gallup Report.* Report No. 206: 3-20.

There is some indication that opposition to busing may be waning. In 1982, roughly three out of ten Americans approved of busing, a number higher than at any time during the 1970s. This increase may reflect experience with busing, since the vast majority of parents with children who had been bused in desegregation plans reported in the early 1980s that they were satisfied with busing.[122]

Two opposing theories have been offered to account for resistance to busing. One explanation suggests that self-interest is at stake: Although the public does not oppose school desegregation, it opposes busing because the perceived costs — e.g., in terms of the loss of neighborhood schools — are considered to exceed the benefits.[123] The other explanation maintains that veiled racism is largely responsible for busing: The public would not go so far as to oppose desegregation outright because open racism is no longer fashionable, yet it feels that Blacks have gone too far and that busing for racial balance is a prime example.[124] Opposition to busing in this view is "symbolic racism" — activity that is justified on a non-racial basis in order to conceal a motivation for "the racial status quo."[125] Although the evidence for either explanation is not definitive, it appears that both operate to create the discrepancy between apparent acceptance of desegregation and rejection of busing as a means to achieve it.[126]

The presence of racial considerations in opposition to busing was recognized and invalidated in a 1982 case in which the Supreme Court confronted an initiative measure adopted by a state's voters. The initiative provided that a school board could not compel a student to attend any school other than that nearest or next nearest his/her home except in specific circumstances (for example, where assignment to a more distant school was needed to secure special education or to avoid health and safety hazards). While no attempt was made to restrict the ability of courts to order busing, the measure was found to violate the guarantee of equal protection. The Court acknowledged that the mere alteration of desegregation policies and laws was not inherently unconstitutional, but the initiative here was designed to deter busing aimed specifically at promoting racial integration and thus created an inherently suspect racial classificaion. The initiative, it was stressed, permitted local school boards to bus students for reasons other than school integration, and it placed in the hands of the state legislature or electorate the decision regarding mandatory busing for school integration even though every other type of student assignment was the responsibility of the local board. The initiative, in short, required that busing intended to promote school integration be treated in a manner that differed from other school-related issues; the manner in which such busing decisions were to be made in the political arena, moreover, reduced the likelihood they could be made at all.

> The initiative removes the authority to address a racial problem — and only a racial problem — from the existing decision-making body, in such a way as to burden minority interests. Those favoring the elimination of de facto school segregation now must seek relief from the state legislature, or from the statewide electorate. Yet authority over all other student assignment decisions, as well as over most other areas of educational policy, remains vested in the local school board.... [T]he community's political mechanisms are modified to place effective decisionmaking authority over a racial issue at a different level of government. In a very obvious sense, the initiative thus disadvantages those who would benefit from laws barring de facto desegregation....[127]

The sensitivity of constitutional philosophy with regard to race does not mean, however, that integration is the responsibility of and must be arranged by government under all conditions. When government action is not the cause of school segregation, there is no constitutional requirement that integration be mandated by government. Accordingly, the equal protection guarantee is not violated by the occurrence of re-segregation — racially-distinct schools that emerge after public policies have corrected a condition of segregation induced by government — where the re-segregation stems from migration patterns for which government is not responsible.[128] Furthermore, the judiciary is not empowered by the Constitution to order a regional integration plan involving multiple school districts where just a single district suffers segregation caused by government and the acts of that district have not promoted segregation in the other districts.[129] The equal protection guarantee is a restraint on goverment; it is only the action of government that can violate this guarantee and justify judicially ordered corrective measures; and the measures permitted can go no further than the problems directly traceable to such action.

Government action designed to rectify the effects of prior discrimination in the context of education can be examined in one final form — affirmative action in admissions to academic programs. The Supreme Court has attempted to answer the constitutional question regarding affirmative action in admissions policies only once.[130] Its decision involved a medical school at a state university which reserved 16 of the 100 seats in each entering class for members of racial and ethnic minority groups. In response to a challenge by a White person claiming that the policy violated the guarantee of equal protection, the Court held in 1978 that minority group membership may play a role in admissions decisions, but it could not fully agree on the manner in which such membership may be employed in the decision-making process. Four members of the Court argued that a policy that sets aside some places in an entering class for minority group members was constitutionally acceptable if its purpose was to eliminate the disproportionate impact resulting from prior discrimination that those groups would suffer without the policy. A fifth member of the Court refused to endorse policies reserving seats on the basis of minority group membership alone but felt that group membership could be employed as one factor among others in decisions on admissions; membership in a minority group could not be a prerequisite to the assignment of places in an entering class, but it could be considered with other factors in the decision-making process. This view allows group membership to be a less-prominent and less-influential factor in admissions policies than the four members of the Court would have permitted, but it is consistent with their position and was explicitly acceptable to them. It is, accordingly, the only type of admissions policy for minorities that is valid under existing constitutional philosophy.

The question of affirmative action was placed before the public by two polls in 1977, more than a year before the *Bakke* decision. When asked if minorities and women should be accorded "preferential treatment" or whether "ability as determined by test scores" should be the standard for college admission and employment, eight out of ten persons said that ability should be the criterion.[131] A year and a half after the decision, this level was unchanged.[132] "Reverse discrimination" to favor minorities was thus not acceptable to the American public — a view reflected by the Supreme Court.

The *Bakke* holding itself — allowing special consideration for minorities without uncompromising favoritism — also appears to be consistent with public values. In 1978, 1980, and 1982, polls asked Americans whether they "favor affirmative action programs...for blacks provided there are no rigid quotas." Two out of three whites, and nine out of ten blacks, approved such programs in higher education.[133]

Let us summarize the important points suggested by the preceding analysis of constitutional philosophy and public attitudes regarding integration in the context of education. Two points deserve mention.

First, the *Brown* decision was not based on overwhelming public support, a situation that also existed in the area of abortion for *Roe v. Wade*. Nonetheless, in the years prior to *Brown*, attitudes consistent with the philosophy of the decision characterized a significant segment of the public — 40 to 50 per cent as indicated by views toward equal employment opportunity for Blacks and the desegregation of interstate travel. In the years before *Brown*, moreover, those attitudes may have become more prevalent, a phenomenon that also preceded *Roe*.

Second, the length of time needed for social adjustment [134] to a Supreme Court decision seems to be a function of the extent of public support that the decision possesses and the degree of social change that it demands. Where public support is comparatively weak and the degree of change required by a decision is great, social adjustment will be relatively long in coming. In the two major aspects of school desegregation in which public support was not strong and considerable social change was needed — viz., the presence of substantial numbers of minorities in primary and secondary schools and busing to achieve racial balance — social adjustment to the Court's decisions involved a substantial period of time. Ten to 15 years elapsed before public acceptance grew appreciably in these areas. Support for the presence of significant numbers of minorities in schools did not increase markedly until the last half of the 1960s even though *Brown* was decided in 1954. Support for busing did not begin to show a rise until recently, even though the Supreme Court approved the tactic in 1971.

5. Government Preferences for Residents

We now examine another topic implicating migration, a topic that will occupy our attention for the remainder of this chapter. The topic concerns policies of state and local governments that have the purpose and/or effect of taking advantage of the migration patterns of the past and the distribution of population they created, or of influencing migration patterns in the future. In particular, we will be examining legislation by state and local governments requiring that certain individuals residing within their jurisdiction be given access to various items of an economic or political nature that are denied to others. In this section, the distinction drawn is between residents and nonresidents or between established residents and new residents; the criterion for classification here is thus residency or its duration. In the next section, the distinction drawn is between residents who are U.S. citizens and residents who are not citizens in defining eligibility for various items.

Cases dealing with preferences given residents for items of an economic nature occurred occasionally over the years, but their frequency became noticeable commencing with the 1969 Supreme Court decision in *Shapiro v. Thompson*.[135] At issue in *Shapiro* was the policy of several states that residence of one year was a prerequisite to the recipt of welfare benefits. Because of the importance of public financial assistance to indigents, the classification by length of residence that the policy created was viewed by the Court as seriously infringing the constitutionally-protected right of indigent Americans to move to and settle in another state, with the result that the policy could be constitutionally invalid only if it advanced a compelling public interest. Using this test, the policy was deemed to be a violation of the equal protection guarantee. The Court recognized that states are free to restrict the amount of money spent on a program but that, in doing so, they must not invidiously classify people unless constitutional standards are satisfied.

Some of the purposes advanced in support of the policy here were found not to be promoted in fact by the policy. For example, there was no basis for believing the one-year waiting period facilitated the planning of budgets for welfare programs or the determination of the legal residence of welfare recipients. At the same time, there was no question regarding the effectiveness of the policy in achieving its principal purpose, namely, the protection of the fiscal viability of the welfare programs. The policy clearly discouraged the in-migration of persons who were likely to be continuing recipients of public assistance, and it excluded from welfare many persons who had not contributed to the public purse from which they would draw. However, the Court concluded, there was no permissible, let alone compelling, public interest in deterring the entry of indigents or in confining welfare assistance to established residents. Indeed, if eligibility for welfare could be made contingent upon prior tax contributions, new residents could be excluded from all public services, including fire and police protection, and state and local governments could make in-migration difficult or impossible for Americans of every income level. The ability of state and local governments to regulate the entry of new residents with invidious classifications based on wealth and length of residence would in turn permit drastic alterations in the social structure of the United States. Such a result, said the Court, was inconsistent with fundamental philosophical principles of American society.

> [T]he nature of our Federal Union and our constitutional concepts of personal liberty unite to require that all citizens be free to travel throughout the length and breadth of our land uninhibited by statutes, rules, or regulations which unreasonably burden or restrict this movement.[136]

From the Depression years to the 1970s, the public was fairly consistent in believing that government is obligated to take care of the truly needy.[137] *Shapiro,* and the cases following it in the next several years that held waiting periods for various types of public assistance to be unconstitutional,[138] thus reflected long-standing public opinion. What was responsible for the occurrence of *Shapiro* in 1969? Why did the case not emerge until the late 1960s? An answer may be found in the rioting by the poor that took place in the United States in 1965-1969. The riots led to a relaxation of welfare eligibility standards by the federal government and, in turn, the extension by states of assistance to a substantially larger number of persons. The response to the riots suggests that welfare in its various forms is a societal mechanism for maintaining social stability: "Welfare largely operates as a form of government efforts to recommit a rebellious poor population to the existing social order."[*139*] American society, like others, possesses mechanisms for alleviating social pressures and preserving social harmony; constitutional adjudication is one such mechanism. The decision and philosophy in *Shapiro* can thus be viewed as fulfilling a fundamental societal requirement.

The importance attached to freedom of migration appeared in a very different situation that confronted the Supreme Court in the early 1980s and here, too, constitutional philosophy was designed to protect societal harmony and cohesion. In dispute was an Alaskan statute under which revenue received by the State from oil production was distributed to residents each year using a formula by which the size of the payment was directly proportional to the length of time the recipient had lived in the state.[*140*] Newly-arrived residents thus were paid less than residents of longer duration. In holding that the statute violated the guarantee of equal protection, the Court was disturbed by the attempt to justify the formula as a means of rewarding residents according to their presumed prior contributions to the state. The justification was unacceptable because it would allow diverse governmental activities, including taxation and tuition in public universities, to be measured by length of residence and "would permit the states to divide citizen into expanding numbers of permanent classes."[*141*] Moreover, in the view of five members of the Court — who were precluded from forming the majority because a divergence in reasoning led them to write two separate concurring opinions — the right to travel was implicated by the statute. In one of the concurring opinions, four justices were concerned that

> if each State were free to reward its citizens incrementally for their years of residence, so that a citizen leaving one State would thereby forfeit his accrued seniority, only to have to begin building such seniority again in his new State of residence, then the mobility so essential to the economic progress of our Nation, and so commonly accepted as a fundamental aspect of our social order, would not long survive.[*142*]

Preferences for monetary payments have not been the only focus of litigation. Preferences for jobs have also.

In examining this issue, a distinction must be made between public and private employment. With respect to employment by government, the Supreme Court has held that employees can be required to reside within the political boundaries of their employer. There is some limited evidence that high levels of residency of public employees within a jurisdiction result in more positive perceptions of governmental services,[143] suggesting that a residence requirement is socially beneficial and would have appreciable public support. However, while an insistence upon bona fide residence at the time of and during employment is permissible, an insistence that a person be a resident for a particular period of time prior to employment evidently is not. Differentiating "between a requirement of continuing residency and a requirement of prior residency of a given duration," the Court has rejected the latter but has accepted "the validity of appropriately defined and uniformly applied bona fide residence requirements" for governmental employment.[144]

Moreover, when a state or local government provides the funds for projects performed by private contractors — which funds thus create employment in the private sector — a requirement that at least some of the resulting jobs be given to residents does not interfere with interstate commerce and violate the Commerce Clause. In such a situation, the state or local government is a participant in the market and, like other participants, need not be concerned that it is burdening interstate commerce; only when it acts as a regulator of the market must the Commerce Clause be considered.[145] Government as a market participant does not inherently affect national economic cohesion; government as a market regulator may.[146] However, the constitutionality of preferences for residents in private employment arising from governmental funds is still uncertain, since it has not been determined if such preferences violate the Privileges and Immunities Clause that "the citizens of each State shall be entitled to all privileges and immunities of citizens in the several States."[147]

The Privileges and Immunities Clause has been used to invalidate an Alaskan statute providing that state residents, if available and qualified, were to be preferred over nonresidents for private sector jobs affected by the production of oil from State-owned land.[148] The statute was found to be unconstitutional because nonresidents were not the cause of the problem (viz., unemployment) it was enacted to solve; unemployment in the state was the result of conditions existing among residents — inadequate skills for and geographic distance from jobs — rather than the entry of nonresidents. Even if nonresidents had been a factor in unemployment, however, the statute was not designed with sufficient precision in its treatment of the problem, because it extended a preferences to all residents rather than just to those who were unemployed.

Three aspects of the opinion of the Supreme Court should be noted. First is its concern with policies giving residents priority for jobs with private employers who do not directly deal with the State. In the statute at issue, the preference was imposed on employers linked to oil production merely through intermediaries. The Court emphasized that a preferences for residents required of employers not directly involved with the State, even if well-designed and effective in reducing unemployment, would encounter a difficult constitutional hurdle, because the Privileges and Immunities Clause provides residents of each State the right to be free from

> discriminating legislation against them by other States; it gives them the right of free ingress into other States, and egress from them; it insures to them in other States the same freedom possessed by the citizens of those States in the acquisition and enjoyment of property... [*149*]

The second aspect of the opinion deserving emphasis is its indication that a policy effective in reducing unemployment that was restricted to private employers dealing directly with the State would have a greater chance of surviving an attack based on the Clause. When government is concerned with its property, it possesses considerable latitude in its conduct. Discrimination against nonresidents is not necessarily valid in such a situation, but it may be.

The third noteworthy aspect of the opinion is that the Privileges and Immunities Clause was applied to the employment preference and invalidated it. The use of the Clause by the Court reflects the belief that employment is important to societal cohesion and that employment discrimination directed at nonresidents jeopardizes that cohesion.

> Some distinctions between residents and nonresidents merely reflect the fact that this is a Nation composed of individual states, and are permitted; other distinctions are prohibited because they hinder the formation, the purpose, or the development of a single union of those states.[*150*]

In addition to government payments and employment opportunities, fees charged by state governments have been the subject of constitutional litigation. Fees have been challenged when the amounts charged were higher for nonresidents than for residents and when they were higher for new residents than for established residents.

The former situation came before the U.S. Court of Appeals for the Eighth Circuit (which covers Arkansas, Iowa, Minnesota, Nebraska, North Dakota, and South Dakota) in 1969. At issue was a tuition charge at a state university that was higher for nonresident students than for residents.[151] The court concluded that there was no constitutional violation because of the financial support provided the university by residents and their families through taxation. Nonresidents did not significantly underwrite the cost of operating the institution, as did residents, and thus they could be charged a higher tuition in order to cover that cost.

If the pervasiveness and size of tuition differentials in state-supported institutions of higher education are used as indicators, support for them in the public at large must be substantial. In academic year 1974-1975, virtually all state-controlled colleges and universities had a differential[152] and fees for nonresidents in 17 representative states averaged almost three times those for residents.[153]

The second situation involving differential fees involved a one-year waiting period in order to qualify for resident status and its accompanying lower tuition at state universities. The waiting period came before two courts in the early 1970s;[154] in each case, no equal protection violation was found and the Supreme Court affirmed the decision. The courts concluded that the waiting periods were not intended to deter in-migration by nonresidents and that higher education, unlike welfare assistance, is not a necessity of life. Accordingly, the waiting periods did not create a serious infringement of the right to interstate travel [155] and were tested only by whether they were reasonably related to a legitimate public interest. The test was satisfied by the greater financial subsidy of residents to the operating costs of the university; the lower contribution of nonresidents in this regard could be recouped in the form of higher tuition during the first year without violating the guarantee of equal protection.[156] However, a student who is a nonresident during his/her first year cannot be continued in that status and made to pay higher tuition indefinitely unless there is evidence that he/she has not become domiciled in the state (i.e., become physically present with an intent to remain after graduation).[157]

Let us, finally, consider preferences for another type of item available from or regulated by government, a type whose nature differs substantially from those already reviewed. Here we will examine distinctions by duration of residence in terms of eligibility to vote and to hold public office. The items considered previously in this section were in essence economic, but those we now examine are political.

We begin with the 1972 decision of the Supreme Court in *Dunn v. Blumstein*.[158] The case involved a statute declaring that persons who had not resided in the state for one year and in their county for three months at the time of the next election were ineligible to vote. In its opinion, the Court explicitly approved a requirement that a voter be a bona fide resident, but the statute challenged in *Dunn* went beyond such a requirement to impose a waiting period in addition to residency. Because the durational residence requirement denied the right to vote to new residents and was viewed as seriously burdening the right to travel to and relocate in another state, it was tested by the compelling interest standard. The Court concluded that the two interests advanced by the State in support of the statute — the prevention of fraudulent voting by nonresidents and the existence of an electorate informed on local issues — were advanced in an inefficient manner, if at all, by the waiting period. The lengthy durational residence requirement imposed by the statute was simply not necessary to accomplish the interests of the State even if those interests were compelling. Accordingly, the classification it created between new and old residents violated the guarantee of equal protection.

> Durational residence laws impermissibly condition and penalize the right to travel by imposing their prohibitions on only those persons who have recently exercised that right. In the present case, such laws force a person who wishes to travel and change residences to choose between travel and the basic right to vote.[159]

Not all waiting periods in the context of voting and elections are unconstitutional, however. The compelling public interest in the prevention of fraudulent voting by nonresidents can justify a short (e.g., 50-day) waiting period.[*160*] Such waiting periods are implemented by the states through the requirement of prior registration, with registration generally closing 30 days or more before an election. Despite the fact that such a requirement is thought to deter voting and to be at least partially responsible for low voter turnout,[*161*] the public largely believes that some waiting period in the form of prior registration should be required, at least for national elections. A solid majority of those surveyed in 1977 opposed a plan of then-President Jimmy Carter to allow same-day registration and voting as long as some proof of residency — for example, a driver's license — could be presented at the polls.[*162*] At least in its approval of short waiting periods, the Supreme Court appears to reflect the view of the public.

Durational residence requirements for election to public office may also be valid depending upon the length of time and the type of office involved. A residence of seven years may be required for governor and state senator in order to allow candidates and voters adequate time to become familiar with one another.[*163*] A one-year residency can be a prerequisite for election to a city council.[*164*] Waiting periods, even when substantial, thus appear to be acceptable for offices characterized by important policymaking functions. However, a ten-year residency for the position of state auditor has been found invalid because of the limited policymaking power of that office.[*165*]

It is significant that, in cases involving eligibility for public office, there has been a distinct preference for the reasonable basis test on the ground that no fundamental right was involved or that, if involved, it was not seriously infringed. Election to public office has not been held to be a fundamental constitutional right, and in any event waiting periods do not permanently prevent, but only delay, a person from seeking public office. Durational residence requirements thus can severely burden a fundamental constitutional right, invoking the compelling interest standard, only insofar as they affect voting or migration, but their impact on voting and the right to travel has been seen generally as minimal. "Since... the benefit denied is not itself a fundamental right (such as voting) nor a basic necessity of life (such as welfare benefits for the poor), the compelling state interest test is inappropriate."[*166*] The failure to apply the strictest constitutional test to often substantial waiting periods in the context of eligibility for public office, but its application in the context of voting, underscores the lesser social value attached to political activity than to the ballot box.

The public's support of short residency requirements for the receipt of welfare [167] and for voting eligibility, together with its apparent tolerance of residency criteria for public employment and reduced tuition at state-supported institutions of higher education, suggests a willingness to permit government to burden migration to the extent of preventing evils perceived as more serious, for example, welfare and voting fraud, unresponsive job performance by government employees or elected officials, and inequitable benefits to non-taxpayers from tax-supported education. Nevertheless, the public highly values freedom of movement for all citizens.[168] This suggests public support for the Supreme Court in rejecting substantial (e.g., one-year) durational residency requirements for the receipt of public goods, since such requirements are longer than necessary to prevent the more serious social evils.

6. State Preferences for U.S. Citizens

Given that immigration into the United States from other countries has been substantial, it should not be surprising that state governments have attempted to protect citizens and given them preferences over noncitizens residing within their jurisdictions. However, while Congress has virtually unrestricted power over immigration, [169] the latitude possessed by states in discriminating against aliens is limited. For immigrants legally-present in the country, this latitude has been determined with regard to public and private employment and government-provided financial benefits. Aliens who are illegally-present, on the other hand, have been the subject of only one major case. We will examine the preferences given citizens commencing with litigation involving immigrants who are lawfully in the country.

The historic importance of immigration has meant that constitutional issues arose early in case law, particularly with regard to employment. In 1915, the Supreme Court invalidated a state requirement that citizens comprise at least 80 per cent of the work force of an employer having more than five workers.[170] The Court concluded that the requirement deprived aliens of the freedom to work — a freedom emanating from the due process guarantee of liberty — and thus interfered with their ability to move between states even though such interference was not contemplated by the federal government in exercising its power over immigration.

While the constitutionality of state discrimination against aliens arose occasionally in earlier years, a substantial body of case law developed starting in the early 1970s. At that time the Supreme Court concluded that classifications based on citizen/alien status were suspect constitutionally when they were directed at employment in the private sector and that they were thus to be tested by the compelling interest standard.[171] Among the various preferences that state governments have provided citizens over aliens, "it is with respect to this kind of discrimination that the States have had the greatest difficulty in persuading this Court that their interests are substantial and constitutionally permissible, and that the discrimination is necessary for the safeguarding of those interests."[172] When faced with a statute requiring that civil engineers in private employment be U.S. citizens, for example, the Court found a violation of the equal protection guarantee. In its opinion, the governmental desire to raise the income and standard of living of engineers by limiting their number was seen as possessing some legitimacy, but the manner in which the interest was advanced was considered not to be the most direct and efficacious possible. "To uphold the statute on the basis of broad economic justification of this kind would permit any State to bar the employment of aliens in any or all lawful occupations."[173] While a State may act to improve the income of its residents, it may not do so by excluding non-citizens who have been legally admitted into the country from employment in the private sector.

Constitutional philosophy as it has developed since the early 1970s with regard to employment preferences for citizens reflects a distinction between the economic functions of society, on the one hand, and its governmental-political functions, on the other.[174] The severity of the standard of constitutionality applied to a State preference for citizens is contingent upon the category into which the employment falls. The exclusion of aliens will be subject to the compelling interest standard when the State is merely regulating economic activity, which it is doing when the exclusion is directed toward employment in the private sector. Even a citizenship requirement for employment in the public sector will be subject to this standard when it is based solely on economic considerations.

However, the lenient standard — which requires only that the governmental action be reasonably related to a legitimate public interest — will be utilized for public employment that involves the governmental functions of the State. Elective or appointive public positions, when limited to citizens, are subject to the reasonable basis test if they entail "the formulation, execution, or review of broad public policy."[175] For example, the exclusion of non-citizens from the competitive civil service has been evaluated under the compelling interest standard and found unconstitutional on the ground that the complete disqualification of aliens was economic in nature.[176] However, the exclusion of non-citizens from serving as police officers,[177] deputy probation officers,[178] and public school teachers [179] was reviewed under the reasonable basis standard and upheld on the ground that the positions involved appreciable discretion in the application of important values of American society. Police officers, in enforcing the law, carry the authority to arrest and enter areas normally considered private; probation officers, in supervising those conditionally released from imprisonment, possess considerable power to control the lives of others and determine whether they can continue their freedom; public school teachers, in their presentation of course materials and in the role-models they create, influence the attitudes of students toward the structure and operation of government and the duties of citizens. The occupants of such public positions must reflect and be sensitive to American ideals and traditions if the institutions essential to society are to be maintained.

States have given preference to U.S. citizens not only in terms of employment but also in terms of government-provided financial benefits. Since only an economic issue is implicated, the compelling interest standard has been applied to the preferences, with the virtually inevitable result that they have been invalidated. In 1971, the Supreme Court ruled that non-citizens cannot be disqualified from welfare assistance;[180] In 1977, the Court held that grants and loans to students in institutions of higher education cannot be limited to citizens or even to aliens who intend to become citizens.[181] In each case, the Court was bothered by the fact that aliens pay taxes and contribute to the economic improvement of the state; they have therefore helped develop the very financial resources from which they are excluded.

> Resident aliens are obligated to pay their full share of the taxes that support the assistance program. There thus is no real unfairness in allowing resident aliens an equal right to participate in programs to which they contribute on an equal basis.[182]

The invalidation of state economic restrictions on aliens that commenced in the early 1970s is on the surface inconsistent with an increasingly prevalent public belief that immigration should be numerically reduced. As Table 4-10 shows, a reduction in immigration attracted increasing support starting in the mid-1960s. A society characterized by rising opposition to future immigration would not seem inclined to eliminate restrictions on already-present aliens. However, both the growing resistance to immigration and the invalidation of restrictions on aliens apparently stem from a common source. The two have arisen because society has gone far in its assimilation of the large volume of immigrants who came to the United States in the first quarter of the twentieth century.[183] To such a society, immigration in the future is of diminished importance and commitment, and opposition to it is more likely.

Table 4-10. Public Attitudes toward Immigration in the U. S.

	Question: Should immigration be kept at its present level, increased or decreased?	Question: On the whole, would you say that you would like to see the number of immigrants allowed to enter our country (U.S.) increased, or would you like to see the number decreased, or do you think that we are letting in the right number?	
	1965*	1977**	1982***
Decreased	33%	42%	66%
Held Steady	39%	37%	23%
Increased	8%	7%	4%
No Opinion/ Not sure	20%	14%	7%
	100%	100%	100%

SOURCES: * George H. Gallup (1972). *The Gallup Poll, Public Opinion: 1935-1971*, v. 3, *1959-1971*. New York: Random House, at 1953.
    ** George H. Gallup (1978). *The Gallup Poll, Public Opinion: 1972-1977*, v. 2, *1976-1977*. Wilmington, DE.: Scholarly Resources, at 1050.
    *** "Opinion roundup: A nation of immigrants" (1982). *Public Opinion* 5 (June/July): 34.

At the same time, assimilation created social homogeneity, erasing distinctions on the basis of alienage and ethnicity. Assimilation resulted from the social and economic mobility of immigrants — attributable in large part to increased use of educational institutions[184] — which reduced residential segregation between ethnic groups.[185] The impact of ethnic background on divisions over political questions thus fell appreciably between the early 1950s and the late 1960s[186] — the period immediately preceding the decisions of the Supreme Court striking down economic discrimination against aliens. "[T]he passage of generations weakens both the importance of ethnic identity and the relevance of that identity for political issues."[187] By 1970, alienage and ethnicity had waned as recognized criteria in American society, making legal distinctions based on those criteria socially intolerable. The stringent constitutional standard for and invalidation of economic discrimination against aliens was the result.

The sociological process of concern here seems to have had an additional consequence for constitutional philosophy. The reduced level of social diversity from assimilation apparently permitted the use of the less stringent test of constitutionality for, and the acceptance of, the exclusion of aliens from employment involving governmental functions. By the late 1970s, assimilation had lessened the social importance of nationality and clarified the central values of American society to the point where a philosophy protecting those values would be socially functional and could be institutionalized. Institutionalization was promoted at that time by an immigrant stream that for the preceding decade had come primarily from Latin America and Asia, areas of a very different cultural nature than those supplying the bulk of immigrants in earlier years.[188] Institutionalization preserves cultural values,[189] and constitutional philosophy was a means for institutionalization to occur.

Let us, finally, consider discrimination against aliens who are illegally-present in the United States. The number of such aliens is substantial; approximately four million Mexicans alone were unlawfully in the U.S. in 1980.[190] The dimensions of the problem led the State of Texas to exclude the children of illegal aliens from public schools, an action that the Supreme Court held violated the equal protection guarantee.[191] The exclusion policy was assessed under the intermediate standard of constitutionality, which requires that the governmental action be substantially related to the advancement of an important public interest in order to be valid. The intermediate test, rather than the less-stringent reasonable basis test, was adopted because the exclusion policy affected children, who were not responsible fo their presence in the country and because the failure to provide education in basic academic skills deprived children of even the opportunity to improve themselves and make a satisfactory adjustment to the demands of modern society. In applying the test, the Court concluded that the policy was not effectively deterring the entry of illegal aliens into the state or improving the quality of education for those lawfully present — interests that might be acceptable under some conditions. Moreover, because many of the children would remain in the country indefinitely, the State was seen as creating a permanent caste, a prospect that appeared particularly disturbing to the Court.

> It is difficult to understand precisely what the State hopes to achieve by promoting the creation and perpetuation of a subclass of illiterates within our boundaries, surely adding to the problems and costs of unemployment, welfare, and crime.... The existence of such an underclass presents most difficult [constitutional] problems for a Nation that prides itself on adherence to principles of equality under law.[192]

The invalidation of the exclusion policy appears quite consistent with trends in public opinion. Between 1977 and 1982, when the Supreme Court rendered its decision, the public was characterized by increasing acceptance of illegal aliens. By the time of the decision, as indicated in Table 4-11, one out of three Americans had come to oppose a prohibition on the employment of illegal aliens. A similar threshold for the invalidation of legislation was found in dealing with fertility-related issues in the preceding Chapter II.

Table 4-11. Percentages Favoring and Opposing Legislation Making Employment of Illegal Aliens Unlawful in the U. S.

	1977		1982**
	March*	Sept.*	
Favor	82%	72%	65%
Oppose	14%	23%	35%
No Opinion	4%	5%	-
	100%	100%	100%

SOURCES: * George H. Gallup (1978). *The Gallup Poll, Public Opinion: 1972-1977*, v. 2, *1976-1977*. Wilmington, DE.: Scholarly Resources, at 1049 and 1213.
 ** "Public opinion referendum" (1982). *The Gallup Report,* Report No. 206: 3-20.

7. Conclusion

As the reader probably has noticed, this chapter has had a number of areas where the social forces responsible for constitutional philosophy were not identified. In none of the chapters were those forces as fully and definitively described as ideally as they should have been, because sociological research has not as yet concerned itself with the link between constitutional philosophy and its societal context. In all of its chapters, accordingly, this book has of necessity been exploratory and tentative in nature. However, the ability to suggest at least some of the relevant social forces has been less with regard to migration and population distribution than with regard to either fertility or mortality. The situation appears to have arisen in large measure because sociologists have emphasized descriptive research over theory development in their work on migration.[*193*] Hopefully, the deficiency will be rectified in the years to come.

NOTES

1. Peter A. Morrison and Allan F. Abrahamse (1983). "Is population decentralization lengthening commuting distances?" *Population Research and Policy Review* 2:189-206 (see Figure 1).

2. Calculated from Table 6 of Bureau of the Census, U.S. Department of Commerce (1981). "Geographic mobility: March 1975 to March 1980," *Current Population Reports*, Series P-20, No. 368.

3. *Id.*

4. Gordon F. DeJong and Ralph R. Sell (1977). "Population redistribution: migration and residential preferences," *Annals of the American Academy of Political and Social Sciences* 429: 132-144.

5. *Id.* at 133-134.

6. Frank Bryan (1982). "Rural renaissance: America on the move again?" *Public Opinion* 5 (June/July): 16-20.

7. James A. Chalmers and Michael J. Greenwood (1980). "The economics of the rural to urban migration turnaround," *Social Science Quarterly* 61: 524-544.

8. Bryan, *supra*, at 17.

9. Harry K. Schwarzweller (1979). "Migration and the changing rural scene," *Rural Sociology* 44: 7-23.

10. Larry H. Long and Kristen Hansen (1980). "Americans on wheels," *Society* 17: 77-83.

11. Chalmers and Greenwood, *supra*, at 534-539. See also Schwarzweller, *supra*, at 12.

12. Bryan, *supra*, at 19.

13. Chalmers and Greenwood, *supra*, at 538.

14. Bryan, *supra*, at 18.

15. Chalmers and Greenwood, *supra*, at 538.

16. DeJong and Sell, *supra*, at 140.

17. Crandall v. Nevada, 6 Wall. 35 (1868).

18. *Id.* at 48-49 [quoting Taney, C.J., dissenting in The Passenger Cases, 7 How. 282 (1849)].

19. 314 U.S. 160 (1941).

20. *Id.* at 173.

21. *Id.* at 173-174.

22. Louis Harris (1976). "The issue: quality of life," *Harris Survey.* Nov. 8: 1-2.

23. "Public divided on relocating urban poor" (1981). *Gallup Report,* Report No. 188: 32-33.

24. Service Machine & Shipbuilding Corp. v. Edwards, 617 F. 2d 70 (5th Cir. 1980), *aff'd,* 449 U.S. 913 (1980).

25. *See* Dean Milk Co. v. Madison, 340 U.S. 349, 354 n.4 (1951); Brimmer v. Rebman, 138 U.S. 78, 82-83 (1891).

26. United States v. Darby, 312 U.S. 100 (1941).

27. 18 U.S.C. § 1952 (1976).

28. United States v. Herrera, 584 F. 2d 1137 (2d Cir. 1978); United States v. Zizzo, 338 F.2d 577 (7th Cir. 1964), *cert. denied,* 381 U.S. 915 (1965); United States v. Schwartz, 398 F. 2d 464 (7th Cir. 1968), *cert. denied sub. nom.*, Pyne v. United States, 393 U.S. 1062 (1969); United States v. Nichols, 421 F.2d 570 (8th Cir. 1970); Turf Center, Inc. v. United States, 325 F.2d 793 (9th Cir. 1963); United States v. Villano, 529 F2d 1046 (10th Cir. 1976), *cert. denied,* 426 U.S. 953 (1976).

29. Caminetti v. United States, 242 U.S. 470 (1917).

30. United States v. Hill, 248 U.S. 420 (1919).

31. 15 U.S.C. § 1691 (1976). See Mourning v. Family Publications Service, Inc., 411 U.S. 356, 377 (1973) regarding the statute's Commerce Clause foundation.

32. 42 U.S.C. § 2000-e (1976); 29 U.S.C. § 206(d)(1976).

33. Los Angeles Department of Water and Power v. Manhart, 435 U.S. 702, 707 (1978).

34. Bundy v. Jackson, 641 F.2d 934 (D.C. Cir. 1981); Tomkins v. Public Service Electric & Gas Co., 568 F.2d 1044 (3rd Cir. 1977); Garber v. Saxon Business Products, Inc., 552 F.2d 1032 (4th Cir. 1977); Hensen v. City of Dundee, 682 F.2d 897 (11th Cir. 1982).

35. Gerdom v. Continental Airlines, Inc., 692 F.2d 602 (9th Cir. 1982), *cert. dismissed,* 103 S.Ct. 1534 (1983); Fernandez v. Wynn Oil Co., 653 F.2d 1273 (9th Cir. 1981); Wigginess Inc. v. Fruchtman, 482 F. Supp. 681 (S.D. N.Y. 1979), *aff'd,* 628 F.2d 1346 (2d Cir. 1980), *cert. denied,* 449 U.S. 842 (1980).

36. Jacobs v. Martin Sweets Co., Inc., 550 F.2d (6th Cir. 1977), *cert. denied*, 431 U.S. 917 (1977); 42 U.S.C. § 2000-e (Supp. V 1981).

37. Hodel v. Indiana, 452 U.S. 314, 324 (1981).

38. "The modern woman, how far has she come?" (1979). *Public Opinion* 2 (January/February): 35-39; see p. 36.

39. Louis Harris (1981). "Support increasing for strengthening women's status in society," *Harris Survey*. Aug. 17: 1-3.

40. Robert V. Robinson and Wendell Bell (1978). "Equality, success, and social justice in England and the United States," *American Sociological Review* 43: 125-143.

41. Bernard Barber (1952). *Science and the Social Order*. Glencoe, IL.: Free Press, at chapter III. *See* Robert K. Merton (1970). *Science, Technology and Society in Seventeenth Century England*. New York: Howard Fertig, at chapter XI.

42. Pamela Barnhouse Walters and Richard Rubinson (1983). "Educational expansion and economic output in the United States, 1890-1969: a production function analysis," *American Sociological Review* 48: 480-493.

43. Robert M. Hauser, Peter J. Dickinson, Harry P. Travis, and John N. Koffel (1975). "Structural changes in occupational mobility among men in the United States," *American Sociological Review* 40: 585-598. Robert M. Hauser and David L. Featherman (1973). "Trends in the occupational mobility of U.S. men, 1962-1970," *American Sociological Review* 38: 302-310.

44. Melvin L. Kohn and Carmi Schooler (1982). "Job conditions and personality: a longitudinal assessment of their recriprocal effects," *American Journal of Sociology* 87: 1257-1286.

45. Mark Baldassare and William Protash (1982). "Growth controls, population growth, and community satisfaction," *American Sociological Review* 47: 339-346.

46. David A. Caputo (1977). "Community size, public attitudes, and population policy preferences," *Urban Affairs Quarterly* 13: 207-222; data from Table 2.

47. "Surveys explore quality of life and managing growth in America," (1974). *Gallup Opinion Index*, Report No. 110: 5-15.

48. Caputo, *supra*, at Table 1 and Table 3.

49. *Id.* at Table 1. See also Charles F. Westoff and James McCarthy (1979). "Population attitudes and fertility," *Family Planning Perspectives* 11: 93-96.

50. *Id.* at Table 1 and Table 2.

51. L.D. Johnson, J.G. Bachman, and P.M. O'Malley (1976 to 1981). *Monitoring the Future*. Ann Arbor, MI.: Institute of Social Research, University of Michigan, at 82, 138, 137, 136, 138, and 138 respectively.

52. E.g., Elizabeth W. Moen (1984). "Voodoo forecasting: technical, political and ethical issues regarding the projection of local population growth," *Population Research and Policy Review* 3: 1-25. Andrew M. Isserman and Peter S. Fisher (1984). "Population forecasting and local economic planning: the technical, legal, and political limits on community control over uncertainty," *Population Research and Policy Review* 3: 27-50. Elizabeth W. Moen (1984). "Population forecasting and planning: some philosophical issues," *Population Research and Policy Review* 3: 51-60.

53. James P. Curry and Gayle D. Scriven (1978). "The relationship between apartment living and fertility for Blacks, Mexican-Americans, and other Americans in Racine, Wisconsin," *Demography* 15: 477-485.

54. Baldassare and Protash, *supra*.

55. Westoff and McCarthy, *supra*.

56. City of Boca Raton v. Boca Villas Corp., 371 So.2d 154 (Fla. Dist. Ct. App. 1979), *cert. denied*, 381 So.2d 765 (Fla. 1980), *cert. denied*, 449 U.S. 824 (1980). *Accord*, City of Boca Raton v. Arvida Corp. 371 So.2d 765 (Fla. 1980), *cert. denied*, 449 U.S. 824 (1980).

57. City of Boca Raton v. Boca Villas Corp., 371 So.2d at 157 [quoting the Supreme Court of Florida in Burritt v. Harris, 172 So.2d 820, 823 (Fla. 1965)]. The rule stated is one generally prevailing in the United States. Patrick J. Rohan (1982). *Zoning and Land Use Controls*. v. 1. New York: Mathew Bender, at 1-83. E.C. Yokley (1978). *Zoning Law and Practice*, 4th ed. v. 1. Charlottesville, VA.: Michie Co., at 65.

58. Charles v. Diamond, 360 N.E.2d 1295 (N.Y. 1977); Robinson v. City of Boulder, 547 P.2d 228 (Colo. 1976).

59. Charles v. Diamond, 360 N.E.2d at 1300.

60. Agins v. City of Tiburon, 447 U.S. 255 (1980). *Cf.* Robert E. Kurzius, Inc. v. Incorporated Village of Upper Brookville, 434 N.Y.S.2d 180, 414 N.E.2d 680 (1980).

61. 447 U.S. at 261.

62. National Land and Investment Co. v. Kohn, 215 A.2d 597 (Pa. 1965). *Accord*, Board of County Supervisors v. Carper, 107 S.E.2d 390 (Va. 1959).

63. 215 A.2d at 612.

64. *Id.* at 611.

65. K.R. Tremblay, Jr., D.A. Dillman, and K.D. Van Liere (1980). "An examination of the relationship between housing preferences and community-size preferences," *Rural Sociology* 45: 509-519.

66. "Surveys explore quality of life and managing growth in America," (1974). *Gallup Opinion Index*, Report No. 110: 5-15. Quote from p. 7.

67. *Id.* at 8.

68. For New Jersey, see Southern Burlington County NAACP v. Township of Mount Laurel, 336 A.2d 713 (N.J. 1975), *cert. denied*, 423 U.S. 808 (1975); Oakwood at Madison, Inc. v. Township of Madison, 371 A.2d 1192 (N.J. 1977); *see* Pascack Ass'n, Ltd v. Mayor and Council of Township of Washington, 379 A.2d 6 (N.J. 1977). For New York, see Berenson v. Town of New Castle, 378 N.Y.S.2d 672 (1975). For Pennsylvania, see Township of Willistown v. Chesterdale Farms, Inc., 341 A.2d 466 (Pa. 1975); Surrick v. Zoning Hearing Board, 382 A.2d 105 (Pa. 1978).

69. Berenson v. Town of New Castle, 378 N.Y.S.2d at 681. *Accord*, Associated Home Builders v. City of Livermore, 557 P.2d 473 (Cal. 1976).

70. Rogin v. Bensalem Township, 616 F.2d 680 (3d Cir. 1980).

71. *Id.* at 688, quoting the U.S. Supreme Court in Village of Belle Terre v. Boraas, 416 U.S. 1, 9 (1974).

72. Malmar Associates v. Board of County Commissioners, 272 A.2d 6 (Md. 1971).

73. Village of Belle Terre v. Boraas, 416 U.S. 1 (1974).

74. Moore v. City of East Cleveland, Ohio, 431 U.S. 494 (1977).

75. Construction Industry Association v. City of Petaluma, 522 F.2d 897 (9th Cir. 1975), *cert. denied*, 424 U.S. 934 (1976).

76. Golden v. Planning Board of the Town of Ramapo, 285 N.E.2d 291 (N.Y. 1972), *appeal dismissed*, 409 U.S. 1003 (1972).

77. *Id.* at 302.

78. Albert Hunter (1974). "Community change: a stochastic analysis of Chicago's local communities, 1930-60," *American Journal of Sociology* 79: 923-947. Harvey M. Choldin, Claudine Hanson, and Robert Bohrer (1980). "Suburban status instability," *American Sociological Review* 45: 972-983.

79. Ralph B. White (1982). "Family size composition differentials between central city-suburb and metropolitan-nonmetropolitan migration streams," *Demography* 19: 29-36.

80. The extent of economic mobility in the United States is considerable, even over a short period of time. Greg J. Duncan (1984). *Years of Poverty, Years of Plenty*. Ann Arbor, MI.: Institute for Social Research, University of Michigan (see pp. 12-14). *See generally* Avery M. Guest, Barrett A. Lee, and Lynn Staeheli (1982). "Chaning locality identification in the metropolis: Seattle, 1920-1978," *American Sociological Review* 47: 543-549.

81. Robert V. Robinson and Wendell Bell, *op. cit.*, quotation from p. 141. Wayne M. Alves and Peter H. Rossi (1978). "Who gets what? Fairness judgments of the distribution of earnings," *American Journal of Sociology* 84: 541-564. Guillermina Jasso and Peter H. Rossi (1977). "Distributive justice and earned income," *American Sociological Review* 42: 639-651.

82. Emily F. Reed (1982). *Exclusionary Zoning and the Urban Ecology in Springfield, Massachusetts*. Unpublished Ph.D. dissertation, University of Massachusetts. Anne B. Shlay and Peter H. Rossi (1981). "Keeping up the neighborhood: estimating net effects of zoning," *American Sociological Review* 46: 703-719.

83. Differences in income between Blacks and Whites narrowed during the 1970s in spite of the severe recession that characterized that period, just as they had during the prosperity of the preceding decade. Reynolds Farley (1977). "Trends in racial inequalities: Have the gains of the 1960s disappeared in the 1970s?" *American Sociological Review* 42: 189-208. Greg J. Duncan and Saul D. Hoffman (1981). "Dynamics of wage change," in Martha S. Hill, Daniel H. Hill, and James N. Morgan (editors), *Five Thousand American Families — Patterns of Economic Progress*. v. IX. Ann Arbor, MI.: Institute for Social Research, University of Michigan. Gordon Green and Edward Welniak (1982). *Changing Family Composition and Income Differentials*. CDS-80-7. Washington, DC.: Bureau of the Census, U.S. Department of Commerce. The proportion of the population that is impoverished, however, is a function of general economic conditions. Lynn G. Zucker and Carolyn Rosenstein (1981). "Taxonomies of institutional structure: dual economy reconsidered," *American Sociological Review* 46: 869-884. Charles A. Murray (1982). "The two wars against poverty: economic growth and the Great Society," *Public Interest*, No. 69 (Fall): 3-16. *But cf.* Judith Treas (1983). "Trickle down or transfers? Postwar determinants of family income inequality," *American Sociological Review* 48: 546-559. The fact that indigents are dependent on the economy for improvement in their standard of living relative to the more affluent segments of society, but that Blacks are less dependent in this regard relative to Whites, suggests that income is a more sensitive dimension and a more integral part of the stratification system than is race.

84. 429 U.S. 252 (1977).

85. *Id.* at 264-265.

The existence of differential effects may violate a statute, however. Racially disproportionate consequences of zoning decisions are thus forbidden by the Fair Housing Act, 42 U.S.C. § 3601 et seq. (1976). Resident Advisory Board v. Rizzo, 564 F.2d 126 (3d Cir. 1977), *cert. denied*, 435 U.S. 908 (1978); Metropolitan

Housing Development Corp. v. Village of Arlington Heights, 558 F.2d 1283 (7th Cir. 1977); United States v. City of Black Jack, Missouri, 508 F.2d 1179 (8th Cir. 1974), *cert. denied*, 422 U.S. 1042 (1975). The Act is grounded on the prohibition against slavery and its incidents embodied in the Thirteenth Amendment. United States v. Hunter, 459 F.2d 205 (4th Cir. 1972), *cert. denied*, 409 U.S. 934 (1972); United States v. Bob Lawrence Reality, Inc., 474 F.2d 115 (5th Cir. 1973), *cert. denied*, 414 U.S. 826 (1973); Williams v. Matthews Co., 499 F.2d 819 (8th Cir. 1974), *cert. denied*, 419 U.S. 1021 (1974).

86. In recent years, roughly one out of four newly constructed, privately owned, one-family houses has been purchased with financial involvement by an agency of the federal government. Bureau of the Census, U.S. Department of Commerce (1982). *Statistical Abstract of the United States: 1982-83*. 103d. ed. Washington, DC.: U.S. Government Printing Office; date from p. 748.

87. Hills v. Gautreaux, 425 U.S. 284, 297 (1976).

88. Ybarra v. City of the Town of Los Altos Hills, 503 F.2d 250 (9th Cir. 1974). For a contrary position under *state* constitutional principles, see Southern Burlington County NAACP v. Township of Mount Laurel, 456 A.2d 390 (N.J. 1983).

89. In 1981, for example, 23 per cent of White households had an income under $10,000 compared to 32 per cent of Spanish-origin households and 45 per cent of Black households. Bureau of the Census, *supra*, at 430.

90. Resident Advisory Board v. Rizzo, 564 F.2d 126 (3rd Cir. 1977), *cert. denied*, 435 U.S. 908 (1978). *See* Citizens Committee for Faraday Wood v. Lindsay, 507 F.2d 1065 (2d Cir. 1975), *cert. denied*, 421 U.S. 948 (1975).

91. Dailey v. City of Lawton, Oklahoma, 425 F.2d 1037 (10th Cir. 1970).

92. Reed, *supra*. *See* John R. Logan and Mark Schneider (1981). "The stratification of metropolitan suburbs, 1960 to 1970," *American Sociological Review* 46: 175-186.

93. "Surveys chart changes in racial attitudes since '63 'March on Washington'" (1978). *Gallup Opinion Index*, Report No. 160: 21-29; quotes from p. 25. See also Herbert H. Hyman and Paul B. Sheatsley (1964). "Attitudes toward desegregation," *Scientific American* 211 (July): 2-9.

94. "Enduring patterns in American life: a decade of NORC surveys," (1982). *Public Opinion* 5 (October/November): 25-40; data from p. 34. *Cf.* George H. Gallup (1972). *Gallup Poll, Public Opinion 1935-1972*. v. 2. New York: Random House (1967 survey of support for federal open housing legislation reported at p. 2057).

95. 347 U.S. 483 (1954).

96. Plessy v. Ferguson, 163 U.S. 537 (1896).

97. Keith W. Olson (1974). *The G.I. Bill, the Veterans, and the Colleges.* Lexington, KY.: The University Press of Kentucky.

98. Alfred H. Kelly (1964). "The school desegregation case," in John H. Garraty (ed.). *Quarrels That Have Shaped the Constitution.* New York: Harper & Row.

99. Reynolds Farley (1970). "The changing distribution of Negroes within metropolitan areas: the emergence of black suburbs," *American Journal of Sociology* 75: 512-529.

100. Stanley Lieberson (1973). "Generational differences among blacks in the North," *American Journal of Sociology* 79: 550-565.

101. Ronald L. Taylor (1979). "Black ethnicity and the persistence of ethnogenesis," *American Journal of Sociology* 84: 1401-1423.

102. Claude S. Fischer (1975). "Toward a subcultural theory of urbanism," *American Journal of Sociology* 80: 1319-1341.

103. George H. Gallup (1972). *Gallup Poll, Public Opinion: 1935-1971.* v. 1, *1935-1948.* New York: Random House, at 528. "The quarter's polls," (1947). *Public Opinion Quarterly* 10 (Spring): 104-139.

104. Mildred Strunk (1947-48). "The quarter's polls," *Public Opinion Quarterly* 11: 639-683.

105. William C. Berman (1970). *The Politics of Civil Rights in the Truman Administration.* Columbus, O.: Ohio State University Press, at 84.

106. Morgan v. Virginia, 328 U.S. 373 (1946). *Morgan* itself rested on substantial public support. In 1942, 44 per cent of all Whites in the United States, and 57 per cent of White outside the South, approved integration of streetcars and buses. Herbert H. Hyman and Paul B. Sheatsley, *supra.*

107. Kelly, *supra*, at 253-254.

108. Olson, *supra*, at 74.

109. Missouri ex rel. Gaines v. Canada, 305 U.S. 337 (1938).

110. Sipuel v. University of Oklahoma Board of Regents, 332 U.S. 631 (1948); Sweatt v. Painter, 339 U.S. 629 (1950).

111. Wayne H. Holtzman (1956). "Attitudes of college men toward non-segregation of Texas schools," *Public Opinion Quarterly* 20: 559-569.

112. Mildred A. Schwartz (1967). *Trends in White Attitudes Toward Negroes.* Chicago: National Opinion Research Center, at 23, 24.

113. 347 U.S. 483, 495 (1954).

114. A. Wade Smith (1981). "Tolerance of school desegregation, 1954-77," *Social Forces* 59: 1256-1274. *See also* A. Wade Smith (1981). "Racial tolerance as a function of group position," *American Sociological Review* 46: 558-573.

115. *Id.*

116. Cooper v. Aaron, 358 U.S. 1, 7 (1958).

117. George H. Gallup (1972). *Gallup Report, Public Opinion: 1935-1971.* v. 2, *1949-1958*, at 1402, 1420, 1563, 1566-7, 1568. v. 3, *1959-1971*, at 1724, 1768, 2210, 2240. New York: Random House.

118. W.A.V. Clark (1982). "Judicial intervention as policy: impacts on population distribution and redistribution in urban areas in the United States," *Population Research and Policy Review* 1: 79-100. Vivian Z. Klaff (1982), "Metropolitan school desegregation: impact on racial integration of neighborhoods in the United States," *Population Research and Policy Review* 1: 259-282.

119. Griffin v. County School Board, 377 U.S. 218, 231 (1964).

120. Green v. County School Board, 391 U.S. 430, 440-441 (1968). *Accord*, Monroe v. Board of Commissioners, 391 U.S. 450 (1968).

121. Swann v. Charlotte-Mecklenburg Board of Education, 402 U.S. 1 (1971).

122. "Majority of parents report school busing has been satisfactory experience" (1981). *Harris Survey*. Mar. 26: 1-3. "Black voting the key to outcome in 1984" (1983). *Harris Survey*. July 21: 1-3.

123. McKee J. McClendon and Fred P. Pestello (1982). "White opposition: to busing or to desegregation?" *Social Science Quarterly* 63: 70-82.

124. John B. McConahay (1982). "Self interest versus racial attitudes as correlates of anti-busing attitudes in Louisville: Is it the buses or the blacks?" *Journal of Politics* 44: 692-720.

125. Steven J. Rosenthal (1980). "Symbolic racism and desegregation: divergent attitudes and perceptions of black and white university students," *Phylon* 41: 257-266.

126. McClendon and Pestello, *supra*, at 79.

127. Washington v. Seattle School District No. 1, 458 U.S. 457, 474-5 (1982).

128. Pasadena City Board of Education v. Spangler, 427 U.S. 424 (1976).

129. Milliken v. Bradley, 418 U.S. 717 (1974).

130. Regents of the University of California v. Bakke, 438 U.S. 265 (1978).

131. "Vast majority against 'affirmative action' for jobs and college openings, ability should be key factor," (1978). *Gallup Opinion Index*, Report No. 151: 6-9.

132. George H. Gallup (1981). *Gallup Poll, Public Opinion 1980*. Wilmington, DE.: Scholarly Resources, at 106.

133. Thomas A. Johnson (1979). "White majority found to favor affirmative action for Blacks if quotas are not rigid," *New York Times*, Feb. 19: A12. Louis Harris (1980). "Americans oppose conservative stances in key social issues," *ABC News-Harris Survey*. Dec. 4: 1-3. Louis Harris (1982). "America is not turning to the right," *Harris Survey*. Aug. 9: 1-3.

134. Cardell K. Jacobsen (1978). "Desegregation rulings and public attitude changes: white resistance or resignation?" *American Journal of Sociology* 84: 698-705. The social adjustment theory maintains that after a court decision, the public will react with increased levels of acceptance, or at least resignation, even when the basis of support prior to the decision was less than majoritarian.

135. 394 U.S. 618 (1969).

136. *Id.* at 629.

137. Hazel Erskine (1975). "The polls: government role in welfare," *Public Opinion Quarterly* 39: 257-274.

138. The principle developed in *Shapiro* has been used to invalidate a one-year residence requirement for non-emergency medical care at public expense, Memorial Hospital v. Maricopa County, 415 U.S. 250 (1974), and two-year and five-year residence requirements for public housing, Cole v. Housing Authority, 435 F.2d 807 (1st Cir. 1970); King v. New Rochelle Municipal Housing Authority, 442 F.2d 646 (2d Cir. 1971), *cert. denied*, 404 U.S. 863 (1971).

139. Sanford F. Schram and J. Patrick Turbett (1983). "Civil disorder and the welfare explosion: a two-step process," *American Sociological Review* 48: 408-414; quotation from p. 413.

140. Zobel v. Williams, 457 U.S. 55 (1982).

141. *Id.* at 64.

142. *Id.* at 68 (Brennan, Marshall, Blackmun, and Powell, JJ., concurring). The majority opinion indicates that the right to travel is involved here but does not analyze the statute from the perspective of this right. *Id.* at 60 n.6.

143. Dennis C. Smith (1980). "Police attitudes and performance: the impact of residency," *Urban Affairs Quarterly* 15: 317-334.

144. McCarthy v. Philadelphia Civil Service Commission, 424 U.S. 645, 647 (1976).

145. White v. Massachusetts Council of Construction Employers, 103 S.Ct. 1042 (1983).

146. *See* Hughes v. Alexandria Scrap Corp., 426 U.S. 794 (1976), especially the concurring opinion of Mr. Justice Stevens beginning at 814.

147. *Id.* at 1048 n. 12. The Privileges and Immunities Clause under discussion here is a provision of Article IV, § 2 of the Constitution. It differs from the Clause of the same name that appears in the Fourteenth Amendment and that provides "no State shall make or enforce any law which shall abridge the privileges or immunities of citizens of the United States." The latter was considered in the section on "Migration Across State Lines" earlier in this chapter.

148. Hicklin v. Orbeck, 437 U.S. 518 (1978).

149. *Id.* at 524, quoting the opinion of the Court in Paul v. Virginia, 8 Wall. 168, 180 (1869).

150. Baldwin v. Montana Fish and Game Commission, 436 U.S. 371, 383 (1978).

151. Johns v. Redeker, 406 F.2d 878 (8th Cir. 1969), *cert. denied sub. nom.*, Twist v. Redeker, 396 U.S. 853 (1969).

152. Cliff K. Travis (1974). "Striking a balance: Indiana's response," *State Government* 47: 233-236.

153. Virginia G. Cook (1974). "A question of residency," *State Government* 47: 226-233.

154. Starns v. Malkerson, 326 F.Supp. 234 (D. Minn. 1970)(three-judge court), *aff'd*, 401 U.S. 985 (1971). *Accord*, Sturgis v. State, 368 F.Supp. 38 (W.D. Wash. 1973)(three-judge court), *aff'd*, 414 U.S. 1057 (1973).

155. Memorial Hospital v. Maricopa County, 415 U.S. 250, 259 (1974).

156. The Privileges and Immunities Clause was not examined in these decisions. However, the Clause is implicated only by state conduct that threatens to disrupt the harmony of the Nation. Baldwin v. Montana Fish and Game Commission, 436 U.S. 371 (1978). Unlike preferences for residents in employment — which have an immediate impact on the ability of individuals to support themselves — a one-year tuition differential at institutions of higher education is unlikely to undermine national cohesion.

157. Vlandis v. Kline, 412 U.S. 441 (1973).

158. 405 U.S. 330 (1972).

159. *Id.* at 342.

160. Marston v. Lewis, 410 U.S. 679 (1973).

161. James MacGregor Burns, J.W. Peltason, and Thomas E. Cronin (1981). *Government by the People.* Englewood Cliffs, NJ.: Prentice-Hall, at 228.

162. "Universal election registration opposed" (1977). *Current Opinion* 5: 92.

163. Chimento v. Stark, 353 F. Supp. 1211 (D. N.H. 1973)(three-judge court), *aff'd*, 414 U.S. 802 (1973); Sununu v. Stark, 383 F. Supp. 1287 (D. N.H. 1974)(three-judge court), *aff'd*, 420 U.S. 958 (1975).

164. City of Akron v. Bell, 660 F.2d 166 (6th Cir. 1981).

165. Antonio v. Kirkpatrick, 579 F.2d 1147 (8th Cir. 1978).

166. City of Akron v. Bell, 660 F.2d 166, 169 (6th Cir. 1981)

167. Jon P. Alston and K. Imogene Dean (1972). "Socioeconomic factors associated with attitudes toward welfare recipients and the causes of poverty," *Social Service Review* 46: 13-23.

168. Louis Harris (1976). "The issue: quality of life," *Harris Survey.* Nov. 8: 1-2.

169. Fiallo v. Bell, 430 U.S. 787 (1977).

170. Truax v. Raich, 239 U.S. 33 (1915).

171. In re Griffiths, 413 U.S. 717 (1973).

172. Examining Board v. de Otero, 426 U.S. 572, 693 (1976).

173. *Id.* at 605-6.

174. Cabell v. Chavez-Salido, 454 U.S. 432 (1982).

175. Sugerman v. Dougall, 413 U.S. 634, 647 (1973).

176. *Id.*

177. Foley v. Connelie, 435 U.S. 291 (1978).

178. Cabell v. Chavez-Salido, 454 U.S. 432 (1982).

179. Ambach v. Norwick, 441 U.S. 68 (1979).

180. Graham v. Richardson, 403 U.S. 365 (1971).

181. Nyquist v. Mauclet, 432 U.S. 1 (1977).

182. *Id.* at 12.

183. Richard D. Alba and Mitchell B. Chamlin (1983). "A preliminary examination of ethnic identification among whites," *American Sociological Review* 48: 240-247. Richard D. Alba (1976). "Social assimilation among American Catholic national-origin groups," *American Sociological Review* 41: 1030-1046.

184. John H. Ralph and Richard Rubinson (1980). "Immigration and the expansion of schooling in the United States," *American Sociological Review* 45: 943-954.

185. Douglas S. Massey (1979). "Effects of socioeconomic factors on the residential segregation of blacks and Spanish-Americans in U.S. urbanized areas," *American Sociological Review* 44: 1015-1022. Douglas S. Massey (1981). "Social class and ethnic segregation: a reconsideration of methods and conclusions," *American Sociological Review* 46: 641-650.

186. David Knoke and Richard B. Felson (1974). "Ethnic stratification and political cleavage in the United States, 1952-68," *American Journal of Sociology* 80: 630-642.

187. *Id.* at 640.

188. Population Reference Bureau (1982). "U.S. population: Where we are; where we're going," *Population Bulletin*, v. 37, no. 2. Immigrant composition changed because of alterations in U.S. immigration law in 1965. *See generally* Barry R. Chiswick (1983). "An alternative approach to immigration policy: rationing by skill," *Population Research and Policy Review* 2: 21-33.

189. Lynn G. Zucker (1977). "The role of institutionalization in cultural persistence," *American Sociological Review* 42: 726-743.

190. Frank D. Bean, Allan G. King, and Jeffrey S. Passel (1983). "The number of illegal migrants of Mexican origin in the United States: sex ratio-based estimates for 1980," *Demography* 20: 99-109.

191. Plyler v. Doe, 457 U.S. 202 (1982).

192. *Id.* at 230, 219.

193. David F. Sly and Jeffrey Tayman (1980). "Metropolitan morphology and population mobility: The theory of ecological expansion reexamined," *American Journal of Sociology* 86: 119-138.

Chapter V.
State versus Federal Authority

To this point we have been considering situations in which government regulation of the behavior of individuals has been challenged as inconsistent with constitutional restraints imposed on government. The issue has been whether government had authority over the individual under the provisions of the Constitution, but the *level* of government was not in question. We now turn to the latter issue and consider whether the federal government or a state takes priority when both are attempting to regulate an activity. The issue may initially appear to be strictly political in nature, but it has potentially important, though largely unrecognized, sociological ramifications. The extent to which national patterns may be established in economic and social life in America is increased as federal authority is allowed to displace that of the states.[1]. The opportunities for diversity and experimentation, which may be important in developing effective solutions to new social problems, [2] are likely to be reduced as states are subject to centralized controls. On the other hand, the standards for various types of activities in the public and private sectors may be seriously deficient in some areas of the country, to the detriment of overriding national concerns and the general welfare,[3] if the federal government lacks authority over the states.

The issue of federalism — how authority should be distributed between the federal government and the states — surfaced in the public forum in the 1930s, and the public debate concerning it persists to the present.

During the Depression and the Second World War, the public was supportive of centralization of authority in the national government as an immediate solution to these crises. Grave situations called for remedies of a similar magnitude and a strong government to implement them. Thus, in 1936 a majority of the public favored a "theory of government" which would concentrate authority at the federal level rather than in the states.[4] Similarly, in 1941 a majority of the public refused to agree that there was "too much power in the hands of the government in Washington," even though the same public was highly suspicious of "a few rich men and large corporations" and "leaders of labor unions" who were thought to be much too powerful.[5]

In more recent years, however, the public has been fairly consistent in its belief that the federal government has grown too large, that this is an unhealthy balance of power, and that authority should be redistributed in favor of the states because the latter are able to deal more effectively with many domestic problems. The change in public attitudes, and the constitutional philosophy that accompanied it, was probably promoted by increasing population numbers and density in the United States. Human interaction is possible with, and governments can efficiently serve, only limited numbers of people.[6] Population growth thus increases the importance of governments that serve relatively small geographic areas.

A review of public opinion since World War II concerning the distribution of authority between the federal government and the states reveals a wide variety of questions with responses of mostly similar import. In 1957, six in ten persons agreed more with a states' rights position than with the view that more problems should be turned over to "the Government in Washington."[7] As Table 5-1 shows, there has been a distinct and growing preference in the last ten years for local, as opposed to federal, government involvement in the provision of services. Local government is evidently regarded as maximizing institutional responsiveness and individual freedom.

Other examples of the public's dissatisfaction with the expansion of federal authority, especially at the expense of state and local governments, can be cited. In the mid-1970s, the public consistently rated local governments as knowing best what people "think and want," the federal government as being "mostly out of touch with the people," and state goverments as falling somewhere in-between.[8] During the same period, when the public

Table 5-1. Public Attitudes toward Government in the U. S.

Question	Response	Year		
		1973	1976	1981
Local gov't is closer to the people, so as many of the services of gov't as possible should be given to [it].	Agree	72%	71%	82%
	Disagree	19%	18%	15%
	Not sure	9%	11%	3%
		100%	100%	100%

SOURCE: "Big government viewed as a problem for the country, but no desire to see traditional role abandoned" (1981). *The Harris Survey*, March 23: 1-3.

was asked to compare state and federal goverments on such positive and negative values as closeness to, being in touch with, and caring about the people, as well as trustworthiness, efficiency, and corruption, the states were favored by wide margins over the federal government in all areas.[9] When asked to indicate how important the "size of the federal government" was in how they would vote in 1976, seven in ten persons ranked it as somewhat to very important.[10]

1. State Legislatures and Political Representation

The importance of state government to the public has been manifested in constitutional philosophy regarding the structure of state legislatures. The question has arisen whether election districts for such legislatures can differ in terms of population numbers. To the extent that such differences occur, inequality exists in the political impact of voters in different districts. The voters in populous (i.e., urban) districts have less influence on state legislatures than those in other (i.e., rural) districts, with consequences for the roles of local, state, and federal governments in American society. Malapportionment has made state legislatures less than sympathetic to the problems of the cities so that urban officials turned to the federal goverment for aid, thereby enhancing the federal role in local affairs. Malapportionment became not only a question of the relative political worth of the individual voter but a question as well of the authority and importance of state and federal governments in local problems.[11]

The Supreme Court had the opportunity as early as 1946 to consider the problem on constitutional grounds but chose not to do so.[12] During the ensuing decade-and-a-half, the Court continued to reject such opportunities, but in the first part of the 1960s, it relented and held that the equal protection guarantee requires that a state legislature — including both houses if it is bicameral — must be apportioned on the basis of population.[13] State legislatures "should be bodies which are collectively responsive to the popular will," a situation that is possible only if "[a] citizen, a qualified voter, is no more nor less so because he lives in the city or on the farm."[14] The Court appears to have reflected a frequent, though less than majority, view held by the public.[15]

2. Traditional State Functions and Federal Authority

Constitutional philosophy most important to the priority of state *vis-a-vis* federal authority emanates from three U.S. Supreme Court cases — *Maryland v. Wirtz* decided in 1968,[16] *National League of Cities v. Usery* decided in 1976,[17] and *Garcia v. San Antonio Metropolitan Transit Authority* decided in 1985.[18] *Maryland v. Wirtz* upheld the application to state schools and hospitals of the federal Fair Labor Standards Act, a statute establishing the minimum hourly wage to be paid to employees and the premium they are to receive for time worked in excess of 40 hours per week. Eight years later, however, *National League of Cities v. Usery* overruled *Wirtz* and held that States and their political subdivisions were constitutionally immune from the Act. Because the philosophy of *National League of Cities* is important, the case will be considered in some depth.

The Fair Labor Standards Act was an exercise of the authority granted Congress by the Commerce Clause, and no argument was made in *National League of Cities* that the Clause did not provide an adequate constitutional basis for the Act. With regard to the private sector, there was thus no question about the validity of the statute, but with regard to the public sector, the contention — accepted by the Court — was that the application of the Act was prohibited by another constitutional provision, a provision seen to be protecting a principle fundamental to the structure of American society. The principle was that the States are not mere extensions of the federal goverment but, rather, independent entities that perform functions with which federal authority cannot seriously interfere. The principle was found to emanate from the restraints on federal action imposed by the Tenth Amendment, which provides that "the powers not delegated to the United States by the Constitution, nor prohibited by it to the States, are reserved to the States respectively, or to the people."

Because decisions regarding the wages and hours of their employees were viewed as inherent aspects of the sovereignty of States and because the federal requirements on these matters could disrupt critical governmental functions performed by state employees, the extension of the Fair Labor Standards Act to state (and local) governments was held to be constitutionally impermissible. The principle — that the independence of States must be preserved for the execution of their essential functions — was a bar to the Act, because the requirements of the statute threatened to

> significantly alter or displace the States' abilities to structure employer-employee relationships in such areas as fire prevention, police protection, sanitation, public health, and parks and recreation. These activities are typical of those performed by state and local governments in discharging their dual functions of administering the public law and furnishing public services. Indeed, it is functions such as these which governments are created bo provide, services such as these which the States have traditionally afforded their citizens. If Congress may withdraw from the States the authority to make those fundamental employment decisions upon which their systems for performance of these functions must rest, we think there would be little left of the States' separate and independent existence.[19]

Federal authority is virtually unlimited with regard to commerce and related activities in the private sector, but the extension of that authority to state government was found to encounter a barrier stemming from the desire to preserve a social structure in which the States possess important functions and are free to fulfill them. However, before the barrier develops, the Court held that three conditions must exist.[20] First, the federal government must be attempting to regulate the States *per se*. To do so, federal law must require States to undertake specified types of action. The condition was not present in a statute providing that federal standards would be imposed for the reclamation of privately-owned land unless the State developed standards fulfilling federal criteria. In this situation, the State was not forced to act; federal law was being applied to private parties, and the State as such was not being regulated even though its authority might be displaced.[21]

The second condition for the establishment of a Tenth Amendment barrier to federal action was that the governmental activity to be regulated must be an aspect of State sovereignty. The autonomy and power of a State to establish policies must be curtailed for the barrier to arise. A federal law mandating that state energy commissions implement federal regulations may intrude on State sovereignty, but a law requiring them only to consider such regulations does not.[22]

The third condition for the Tenth Amendment barrier was that federal law must significantly reduce the ability of states to determine the manner in which their traditional governmental functions are to be conducted. This condition required (1) a basic function performed by state (or local) government and (2) serious federal interference with the function. With regard to (2), the Supreme Court in 1983, finding no significant intrusion on the ability of States to perform their functions, upheld a federal statute that prohibited States from forcing public employees to retire automatically at an age lower than 70.[23] The statute did not preclude States from retiring employees who were physically unable to perform their duties; it only required them to abandon age criteria for automatic retirement of employees less than 70 years old and use individualized determinations of physical ability unless for particular occupations they could establish that age was a bona fide qualification. The effect of the statute was considered to be minimal both with regard to the financial ability of the States to deliver public services and with regard to their ability to implement broad social and economic policies.

In reaching this decision, the Supreme Court expressed the predispositions of the public regarding mandatory retirement. During the decade prior to the decision, the public was supportive of permitting people to work until they want to retire. As Table 5-2 shows, there was overwhelming, and possibly growing, support for allowing individuals to continue to work as long as they want and are able to do so. At the same time, there was greater resistance to decreases in the mandatory retirement age. These views were reflected by the Court. Moreover, as a comparison of Tables 5-2 and 5-3 indicates, attitudes supporting the right of older Americans to work were more pervasive than attitudes favoring the states *vis-a-vis* the federal government, suggesting the public preferred that federal authority prevent States from forcing early retirement on their employees rather than that States be allowed the freedom to act to the detriment of older workers.

Table 5-2. Public Attitudes toward Mandatory Retirement in the U. S.

Question:	Response	Year			
		1974	1977	1978	1981
Nobody should be forced to retire because of age, if he wants to continue working and is still able to do a good job.	Agree	86%**	86%*	88%***	91%**
	Disagree	12%	12%	10%	9%
	Not sure	2%	2%	2%	-
		100%	100%	100%	100%
The age at which people are required to retire has gotten younger in recent years. Do you think this is a good thing or not?	Agree	45%*	39%*		
	Disagree	40%	51%		
	Not sure	15%	10%		
		100%	100%		

SOURCES:* "'No' vote on forced retirement" (1977). *The Harris Survey*, Sept. 26: 3.
 ** "Work and retirement" (1981). *The Harris Survey*, Dec. 14: 12.
 *** "American attitudes toward persons and retirement" (1979). *Hearing before the Select Committee on Aging, House of Representatives*. 96th Congress, Washington, DC.: U.S. Government Printing Office.

National League of Cities was thus not an insurmountable hurdle to federal regulation of state activities. Social values continued to influence constitutional interpretation, suggesting the existence of a flexible social structure. Flexibility is an accompaniment of complexity — both as a cause and effect[24] — and it was apparently the complexity of society that led the Supreme Court in early 1985 to overrule *National League of Cities*. In *Garcia v. San Antonio Metropolitan Transit Authority*,[25] the Court by a five-to-four vote overturned its prior decision because experience indicated the principle that the Tenth Amendment protects only traditional state functions from federal control could not be applied in a consistent manner. Since the line between traditional and nontraditional governmental functions could not be reliably drawn, it was abandoned. At the same time, however, the importance of preserving the independence of the States from overbearing federal action was explicitly acknowledged. The primary limitation on maintaining State sovereignty was seen by the Court as resting in the

Table 5-3. Support for Strengthened State Governments in the Early 1980s in the United States

1981*

QUESTION: Which theory of gov't do you favor — concentration of power in the federal gov't or...in the state gov'ts?		Which is the more..... ...understanding of the needs of the people?	...likely to administer social programs efficiently?	...likely to make decisions free from political corruption?
Federal	28%	15%	18%	26%
State	56%	67%	67%	42%
Same	-	9%	8%	20%
No opinion	16%	9%	7%	12%
	100%	100%	100%	100%

1982**

QUESTION: All in all would you say the present balance of responsibility between the federal gov't on the one hand, and the state and local gov'ts on the other, is:

Tipped too far toward the federal gov't?	55%
Balanced about right?	24%
Tipped too far toward state and local gov't?	9%
Don't know	12%
	100%

SOURCES: *"The role of government: Public receptive to 'New Federalism'" (1982). *Public Opinion* 5 (February/March): 26-31 (see p. 29).
**"Public values, private initiative" (1982). *The Gallup Report*, Report No. 193: 2-9.

political process, but the majority also concluded that, when the political process fails to block federal policies destructive of this sovereignty, the Constitution will be used to negate federal powers. "Any substantive restraint on the exercise of Commerce Clause powers ... must be tailored to compensate for possible failings in the national political process," wrote the majority, but

> we continue to recognize that the States occupy a special and specific position in our constitutional system and that the scope of Congress' authority under the Commerce Clause must reflect that position.[26]

Although the majority refrained from suggesting the nature of relevant constitutional limitations, it is probable that the Court in future years will develop and impose constraints. Public values appear to exhibit a strong concern with the integrity of the States, and those values are likely to be reflected in constitutional philosophy in the years to come.[27]

It is important to note that the three cases discussed in this section — *Wirtz, National League of Cities,* and *Garcia* — applied to federal action based on the Commerce Clause. Another provision of the Constitution — viz., the Fourteenth Amendment — provides Congress with the authority to enact statutes regulating States that does not apparently encounter a constitutional barrier. Federal legislation prohibiting sex discrimination in public employment is based on the Equal Protection Clause of the Fourteenth Amendment and the express authority given Congress by that Amendment to prohibit States from making distinctions between people.[28] With Supreme Court approval, the legislation thus forbids state and local governments from using gender to calculate premiums for and benefits from retirement programs for their employees.[29] Employees in the public, as well as private, sector cannot be distinguished on the basis of sex in determining their contributions to and benefits from pensions and annuities.

In terms of distinctions involving gender, the philosophy of the federal statute prohibiting employment-related discrimination appears to match that of constitutional philosophy under the Fourteenth Amendment,[30] and the equal protection guarantee of the latter might thus on its own have invalidated a sex-based formula in retirement programs for government employees. As it began the last quarter of the twentieth century, American society was characterized by a readily-identifiable concern with minimizing social distinctions between males and females. It is well-established that mortality rates vary appreciably by sex, but retirement programs must utilize sex-neutral formulas in calculating benefits because of the societal commitment to eliminating all gender identifications other than those reflecting significant biological differences between males and females. In the words of the Supreme Court:

> Practices which classify employees in terms of religion, race, or sex tend to preserve traditional assumptions about groups rather than thoughtful scrutiny of individuals. . . . [Gender-distinct] mortality tables are easily interpreted as reflecting innate differences between the sexes; but a significant part of the longevity differential may be explained by the social fact that men are heavier smokers than women.[31]

The use of gender in employee retirement policies was the subject of two Supreme Court decisions — the first rendered in 1978 and the second in 1983 — but the decisions appeared only after public attitudes toward equalizing the status of men and women had reached a plateau of considerable strength. As Table 4-4 in Chapter IV indicates, two out of three Americans prior to the first decision had come to favor changes that improved the social position of women. This level had increased dramatically since 1970 but underwent virtually no change subsequently. The ideological change, and its manifestations in the Supreme Court decisions, was probably facilitated in turn by the fluid stratification system in the United States[32] and helped to adapt that system to a society characterized by a commitment to individualism, both personal[33] and economic.[34]

NOTES

1. *See, e.g.*, Eviatar Zerubavel (1982). "The standardization of time: a sociohistorical perspective," *American Journal of Sociology* 88: 1-23.

2. *See* Michael K. Moch and Edward V. Morse (1977). "Size, centralization and organizational adoption of innovations," *American Sociological Review* 42: 716-725. *See generally* Robert L. Savage (1978). "Policy innovativeness as a trait of American states," *Journal of Politics* 40: 213-224.

3. *See* Paul Burstein and Margo W. MacLeod (1980). "Prohibiting employment discrimination: ideas and politics in the congressional debate over equal employment opportunity legislation," *American Journal of Sociology* 86: 512-533. Paul Burstein (1979). "Equal employment opportunity legislation and the income of women and nonwhites," *American Sociological Review* 44: 367-391.

4. George H. Gallup (1972). *Gallup Poll, Public Opinion 1935-1971*, v. 1, *1935-1948*. New York: Random House, at 14.

5. *Id.* at 277.

6. G. Edward Stephan and Douglas R. McMullin (1981). "The historical distribution of county seats in the United States: a review, critique, and test of time-minimization theory," *American Sociological Review* 46: 907-917. James Tucker and S.T. Friedman (1972). "Population density and group size," *American Journal of Sociology* 74: 742-749. *Cf.* Patrick D. Nolan (1979). "Size and administrative intensity of nations," *American Sociological Review* 44: 110-125.

7. Gallup, *supra*, v. 2, *1949-1958*, at 1504-5.

8. "Leadership ratings" (1977). *Harris Survey*. Dec. 22: 1-2.

9. "More trust for state government" (1976). *Harris Survey*. July 5: 1.

10. George H. Gallup (1978). *Gallup Poll, Public Opinion 1972-1977*, v. 2, *1976-1977*. Wilmington, DE.: Scholarly Resources, at 879-880.

11. John P. Wheeler and John E. Bebout (1962). "After reapportionment," *National Civic Review* 51: 246-250.

12. Colegrove v. Green, 328 U.S. 549 (1946).

13. Baker v. Carr, 369 U.S. 186 (1962); Reynolds v. Sims, 377 U.S. 533 (1964). See also Gray v. Sanders, 372 U.S. 368 (1963).

14. 377 U.S. at 565, 568. *See also* Burns v. Richardson, 384 U.S. 73 (1966).

15. George H. Gallup (1972). *Gallup Poll, Public Opinion 1935-1971*, v. 3, *1959-1971*. New York: Random House, at 1897-8.

16. 392 U.S. 183 (1968).

17. 426 U.S. 833 (1976).

18. 53 U.S. Law Week 4135, 105 S.Ct. —— (1985).

19. 426 U.S. at 851.

20. Hodel v. Virginia Surface Mining and Reclamation Association, 452 U.S. 264 (1981).

21. *Id.*

22. Federal Energy Regulatory Commission v. Mississippi, 456 U.S. 742 (1982).

23. Equal Employment Opportunity Commission v. Wyoming, 103 S.Ct. 1054 (1983).

24. *See* Melvin L. Kohn and Carmi Schooler (1978). "The reciprocal effects of the substantive complexity of work and intellectual flexibility: a longitudinal assessment," *American Journal of Sociology* 84: 24-52.

25. 53 U.S. Law Week 4135, 105 S.Ct. —— (1985).

26. 53 U.S. Law Week at 4142.

27. In this regard, it should not be overlooked that the majority and minority positions in *Garcia* represented five and four members of the Court, respectively, and that the decision would have been altered by change in a single vote. In the dissent were Justices whose philosophy seems to reflect that of the public and of President Ronald Reagan, who is likely to appoint at least one new member of the Court during his second term of office.

28. United States v. New Hampshire, 539 F.2d 277 (1st Cir. 1976), *cert. denied*, 429 U.S. 1023 (1976); Usery v. Allegheny County Institution District, 544 F.2d 148 (3rd Cir. 1976), *cert. denied*, 430 U.S. 946 (1977); Usery v. Charleston County School District, 558 F.2d 1169 (4th Cir. 1977); Marshall v. Owensboro-Daviess County Hospital, 581 F.2d 116 (6th Cir. 1978); Norris v. Arizona Governing Committee, 671 F.2d 330 (9th Cir. 1982), *aff'd in part and rev'd in part per curiam on other grounds*, 103 S.Ct. 3492 (1983).

The legislation applies to employers in the private sector under the Commerce Clause. *See* 42 U.S.C. §§ 2000e(b)(g)(h), 2000e-2 (a)(1) (1976).

29. City of Los Angeles, Department of Water and Power v. Manhart, 435 U.S. 702 (1978); Arizona Governing Committee v. Norris, 103 S.Ct. 3492 (1983).

30. *Compare* City of Los Angeles, Department of Water and Power v. Manhart, 435 U.S. 702 (1978) *with* Mississippi University for Women v. Hogan, 458 U.S. 718 (1982).

31. 435 U.S. at 709-710. Demographic research, however, apparently does not anticipate a reduction in the mortality rate disparity between males and females. *See* Eileen M. Crimmins (1983). "Recent and prospective trends in old age mortality," paper presented at the annual meeting of the American Association for the Advancement of Science (tables 3 and 4).

32. *See* Moshe Semyonov (1980). "The social context of women's labor force participation: a comparative analysis," *American Journal of Sociology* 86: 534-550.

33. *See* Ron Lesthaeghe (1983). "A century of demographic and cultural change in Western Europe: an exploration of underlying dimensions," *Population and Development Review* 9: 411-435.

34. *See* Fred C. Pampel and Jane A. Weiss (1983). "Economic development, pension policies, and the labor force participation of aged males: a cross-national, longitudinal approach," *American Journal of Sociology* 89: 350-372. *See also* Richard F. Kamalich and Solomon W. Polachek (1982). "Discrimination: fact or fiction? An examination using an alternative approach," *Southern Economic Journal* 49: 450-461.

Chapter VI.
A Look Ahead

Philosphers may argue whether prediction is an essential facet of science, but certainly prediction improves the practical utility of a scholarly endeavor.[1] In the preceding chapters, our concern was with explanation — the identification of the social forces that appeared to account, at least in part, for already-existing court decisions. In this chapter, our concern is with prediction — the delineation of an issue that we believe has a reasonable probability of coming before federal appellate courts in the foreseeable future, of the decision that may be expected by those courts in construing the Constitution, and of the social forces that apparently will foster the decision. If the approach thast has been pursued in prior chapters is to be of maximum utility, it should lead to accurate predictions regarding court decisions that are yet to occur.

Unfortunately, there are a number of factors that seriously constrain our ability to develop predictions having a high degree of accuracy. First, sociology is the principal scientific discipline from which we must draw in order to identify the social forces relevant to court decisions, but like all social sciences, sociology generally is concerned with topics that have already attracted considerable public attention. Such topics, by their very nature, have typically been litigated extensively. Issues regarding which predictions can be made here are thus limited to those few that have been the focus of the public and of sociological research, but not of federal appellate courts.

Second, in spite of its impressive strides in the past decade, sociology is still in the process of developing fully its research capacity and potential data sources. The empirical research required for making sound predictions is accordingly limited, particularly when one is delving into a topic necessitating the construction of a bridge between previously unconnected scholarly endeavors.

Third, the authors are themselves members of the society that they are examining and as such are restricted in their ability to identify the lines along which important social changes will occur. Socialization and involvement in a society make it difficult to recognize central attributes of th social fabric that are likely to be altered.

In spite of these constraints, there is an issue that, we believe, is reasorably likely to reach federal appellate courts within the next ten years and to result in the invalidation of present government policy. The issue is State recognition of marriage between homosexuals. In the first half of the 1970s, three state courts confronted the question and rejected the contention that homosexuals possess a constitutionally-protected right to obtain a marriage license.[2] A full exploration of the question, however, still awaits the federal courts.[3] "Changes that have taken place in sexuality, in sexual conduct and attitudes," it has been argued, "constitute probably the most dramatic and significant transformations of the social world in the present century."[4] There is good reason to believe that the changes are not yet complete and that State acceptance of homosexual marriage will be found to be constitutionally required.

Let us consider the social forces that will probably be influential in altering the social and legal position of homosexuals in the United States. The first is the erosion of religion as an important basis for social distinctions and identification. Homosexuality seems to have been the object of antipathy historically because at least in part it was perceived by religious groups as a threat to their survival.[5] The social importance of religion, however, is weakening. Not only has the incidence of interfaith marriages been increasing,[6] but there has been a decline in religious commitment and traditionalism,[7] erasing if not at least easing conditions linked to hostility toward homosexuality.[8]

The second factor changing the position of homosexuals is the substantial, and increasing, level of urbanization of the American population. In 1980, 64.3 per cent of the population resided in a metropolis of at least 250,000 people, an increase from 60.2 per cent in 1970.[9] Residents of urban areas are more likely to interact with persons of diverse backgrounds and ideas, [10] increasing the incidence of unconventional behavior and reducing the importance of traditional groups and their ideologies.[11] The urban nature of the population helps explain the decline in religious commitment noted above; an urban environment generates, and the deterioration of religion results from, values and conduct characterized by individualism, acceptance of diversity, and non-traditionalism.[12]

Urban conditions appear to act directly to promote acceptance of homosexuality as well as indirectly through their impact on religion. In a study of attitudes toward activities of a sexual nature, it was found that tolerance of homosexuality was associated with residence as an adult in a metropolis having a population of at least one million and especially with residence during the individual's sexually-formative years in an urban area of at least 50,000.[13] Each of the two conditions characterizes a substantial number of Americans. Roughly four out of ten adults resided in a metropolis having at least one million population during the 1970s,[14] and somewhat more than half of all 14-18 year olds lived in an urbanized area of at least 50,000.[15] A large segment of American society is thus subject to the conditions associated with tolerance of homosexuality.

Public attitudes provide concrete evidence supporting the hypothesis that the legal position of homosexuals can be expected to change in the foreseeable future. The last ten years have seen no diminution of the overwhelming view that homosexuality is "wrong",[16] but a substantial proportion of American adults nonetheless believe that homosexual relationships voluntarily undertaken should be accepted legally. National surveys in 1977 and 1982 posed the question, "Do you think homosexual relations between consenting adults should or should not be legal?" Responses were distributed as follows:[17]

	1977:	**1982:**
Should	43%	45%
Should not	43%	39%
No opinion	14%	16%
	100%	100%

The legalization of homosexual relationships is thus now favored by a number approaching half of all Americans, and there may have been some strengthening of that belief between 1977 and 1982. It is also significant that opposition to legalization apparently declined during the period.

Support for the legalization of homosexual relationships — as well as the trend between 1977 and 1982 toward rising support and lessening opposition — was most pronounced among persons with a college education. This group is particularly important because the members of the judiciary — those who construe the Constitution — are selected from it. The distribution of responses by the college-educated to the survey question regarding whether homosexual relations should or should not be legal thus deserves note:[18]

	1977:	1982:
Should	57%	61%
Should not	35%	25%
No opinion	8%	14%
	100%	100%

Favorable attitudes toward legalization in 1982 were manifested by three out of five Americans with a college education, a level that constitutes an influential majority and that had risen slightly since 1977. Primarily because of a decline in unfavorable attitudes, support for legalization among the college-educated in 1982 was two-and-one-half times more frequent than opposition, a disparity far exceeding that in the population as a whole. Favorable attitudes toward legalization, in short, dominate in an important segment of American society.

On the basis of public opinion data analyzed in preceding portions of this book, particularly Chapter II, it is clear that attitudes have now reached the point where the judicial invalidation of prohibitions against homosexual marriage is distinctly possible. The apparently increasing and significant political activism of homosexuals[19] makes it likely that court challenges to those prohibitions will be forthcoming in the near future. Accordingly, the constitutional rationale that courts can follow in striking down legal barriers to homosexual marriage should be briefly outlined.

The most logical approach to the invalidation of prohibitions on homosexual marriage under existing constitutional philosophy appears to lie in the joint use of the equal protection and due process guarantees and the restraints they place on the ability of government to classify persons and regulate their actions. Allowance of opposite-sex, but not same-sex, marriage establishes a classification that involves limits on the freedom to marry, a freedom that is sheltered by the right of privacy. Because of the social value attached to personal liberty, the privacy prerogative has been deemed a fundamental constitutional right, and restrictions that directly and severely impede access to marriage must satisfy the compelling interest test in order to be constitutional.

Since "the right to marry is of fundamental importance for all individuals,"[20] persons of the same sex who seek to marry are evidently within the purview of the constitutional shield, and government refusal to issue them a license is a direct and substantial restriction on their freedom to marry. Given this, the government can prevail only if it demonstrates that its policy advances a compelling public interest and is not unnecessarily broad. It is doubtful that there is adequate evidence to demonstrate that homosexual marriages are a serious threat to society and that the governmental interest in suppressing them is compelling. Permanent homosexual relationships exist without marriage, and it is unlikely that the denial of the legal protections of marriage to them can be shown to provide a societal benefit of overriding importance.

In conclusion, a macro-sociological approach to law has been used in this and the preceding chapters. Law has been viewed as a social institution and, as such, has been assumed to respond directly to change in the properties of society. To this end, societal attributes were examined in an attempt to illuminate the conditions giving rise to constitutional philosophy through court decisions on population-related questions.

The present effort has clearly been exploratory and tentative in nature. But while the conclusions reached here are far from definitive, the effort undertaken suggests that a macro-sociological approach to law holds considerable promise and deserves further attention from empirically-oriented sociologists and legal scholars.[21] The research and statistical tools of sociology have matured and can be fruitfully applied to court decisions as well as to statutes. The actions of judicial and legislative bodies, in short, need to be treated sociologically as dependent variables.

Research in the field of macro-sociology and law, however, will not be without difficulty. One problem is likely to be particularly troublesome. Courts and legislatures have legal jurisdiction over geographic areas that are sociological diverse. A federal district court, for example, can include both rural and urban counties; a circuit of the U.S. Court of Appeals can include states with heterogeneous social conditions.[22] Because of this diversity, the nature of the relationship between the independent variables that have been selected for study and court decisions (and statutes) may prove to be elusive. Measurements of independent variables may necessarily be more complex in macro-sociological research on law than in other types of research endeavor. In assessing the relationship of a given independent variable (e.g., affluence) to a court decision, for instance, researchers may be forced to develop measures of central tendency and variability in the variable for each sociologically-relevant area within the geographic jurisdiction of the court.

The problems confronting empirical investigation in macro-sociology and law, however, should not be permitted to discourage research in this field. A substantial investment of research resources may be necessary to obtain knowledge on the subject, but to the extent that knowledge is available, the benefits can be appreciable. For example, the legal profession will be able to provide the parties to contemplated litigation challenging the constitutionality of a statute with a more accurate estimate of their chance of success, leading to the avoidance of lawsuits.

Macro-sociological research on law, in short, is long overdue.

NOTES

1. Abraham Kaplan (1964). *The Conduct of Inquiry*. San Francisco: Chandler.

2. Baker v. Nelson, 191 N.W.2d 185 (Supreme Court of Minnesota 1971), *appeal dismissed*, 409 U.S. 810 (1972); Jones v. Hallahan, 501 S.W.2d 588 (Court of Appeals of Washington 1974). The latter two decisions were rendered by intermediate appellate courts in their respective states.

3. One of the three decisions was appealed to the U.S. Supreme Court, which dismissed the appeal "for want of a substantial federal question." Baker v. Nelson, 409 U.S. 810 (1972). A dismissal of this nature is a determination of the merits of the issue within the context of the legal principles considered by the lower court. Mandel v. Bradley, 432 U.S. 173 (1977). However, such a dismissal is not binding on lower federal courts in future cases in which legal principles are advanced that were not examined by the court from which the appeal was taken. Thomas L. Phillips, Jr. (1978). "The precedential effect of summary affirmances and dismissals for want of a substantial federal question by the Supreme Court after *Hicks v. Miranda* and *Mandel v. Bradley*," *Virginia Law Review* 64: 117-143. In *Baker*, the originating court did not consider whether the restriction of marriage to persons of the opposite sex was a *serious* intrusion on the right of privacy and, if so, whether the restriction satisfies the most stringent test of constitutionality, i.e., whether it advances a compelling public interest by the narrowest possible means. This test was developed and applied in the context of marriage by the Supreme Court in a decision rendered subsequent to *Baker*. Zablocki v. Redhail, 434 U.S. 374 (1978).

The U.S. Supreme Court itself has in the past reviewed and decided issues that, as in *Baker*, it had previously dismissed summarily. "It is not at all unusual for the Court to find it appropriate to give full consideration to a question that has been the subject of previous summary action." Washington v. Confederated Bands and Tribes, 439 U.S. 463, 477 n.20 (1979). When consideration is given to an issue that has been dismissed for want of a substantial federal question, the Court may well hold the action of a State to be unconstitutional — even if there has been no change in applicable legal principles. ARMCO Inc. v. Hardesty, 104 S.Ct. 2620, 2623 n.7 (1984).

4. Edward A. Tiryakian (1981). "Sexual anomie, social structure, societal change," *Social Forces* 59: 1025-1053; quotation from p. 1038.

5. Christie Davies (1982). "Sexual taboos and social boundaries," *American Journal of Sociology* 87: 1032-1063.

6. Norval D. Glenn (1982). "Interreligious marriage in the United States: patterns and recent trends," *Journal of Marriage and the Family* 44: 555-566.

7. David A. Roozen and Jackson W. Carroll (1979). "Recent trends in church membership and participation: an introduction," in Dean R. Hoge and David A. Roozen (eds.), *Understanding Church Growth and Decline: 1950-1978*. New York: Pilgrim Press.

8. Dean R. Hoge (1979). "National contextual factors influencing church trends," in *id*.

9. Bureau of the Census, U.S. Department of Commerce (1982). *Statistical Abstract of the United States, 1982-83*. 103rd edition. Washington, DC.: U.S. Government Printing Office. Figures calculated from p. 15, table 16.

10. Claude S. Fischer (1975). "Toward a subcultural theory of urbanism," *American Journal of Sociology* 80: 1319-1341. Bruce H. Mayhew and Roger L. Levinger (1976). "Size and the density of interaction of human aggregates," *American Journal of Sociology* 82: 86-110.

11. Peter M. Blau, Terry C. Blum, and Joseph E. Schwartz (1982). "Heterogeneity and intermarriage," *American Sociological Review* 47: 45-62.

12. Dean R. Hoge and David A. Roozen (1979). "Some sociological conclusions about church trends," in Hoge and Roozen, *supra*, at 328. Fischer, *supra*. Mayhew and Levinger, *supra*.

13. G. Edward Stephan and Douglas R. McMullin (1982). "Tolerance of sexual nonconformity: city size as a situational and early learning determinant," *American Sociological Review* 47: 411-415.

14. Bureau of the Census, U.S. Department of Commerce (1978). "Social and economic characteristics of the metropolitan and nonmetropolitan population: 1977 and 1970," *Current Population Reports*, Series P-23, No. 75. Figures calculated from table 1, pp. 20-21, and include persons 18 years of age and older.

15. Bureau of the Census, U.S. Department of Commerce (1973). *1970 Census of Population*. v. 1: *Characteristics of the Population*. Part 1: *United States Summary*. Section 1, at table 52. Bureau of the Census, U.S. Department of Commerce (1983). *1980 Census of Population*. v. 1: *Characteristics of the Population*. Chapter B. *General Population Characteristics*. Part 1: *United States Summary*, at table 43.

16. James A. Davis (1982). *General Social Surveys, 1972-1982: Cumulative Codebook*. Chicago: National Opinion Research Center, University of Chicago, at 163.

17. George H. Gallup (1983). *Gallup Poll, Public Opinion 1982*. Wilmington, DE.: Scholarly Resources, at 255.

18. *Id*. at 254. George H. Gallup (1978). *Gallup Poll, Public Opinion, 1972-77*. v. II, *1976-77*. Wilmington, DE.: Scholarly Resources, at 1151.

19. Rita Beamish (1983). "In politics, gay community is force to be reckoned with," (Wilmington, DE.) *Sunday News Journal* (Dec. 11): A13. Associated Press report.

20. Zablocki v. Redhail, 434 U.S. 374, 384 (1978).

21. *See* Edward W. Lehman (1978). "Sociological theory and social policy," *International Journal of Comparative Sociology* XIX: 7-23.

22. See 28 *United States Code* §§ 41, 81-131 (1982).

Index

Abortion, 31ff.
  consent of spouse, 39
  constitutional issues on funding of, 43f.
  first trimester, attitudes toward, 35
  public funding for, 42f.
Affirmative action, 129
Affluence, effects of, 26
Alaska, 134
Alienage, 143
Aliens, illegal, 144
  state economic restrictions, 142
American judicial system, 6f.
American stratification system, 110
Assimilation, 143
Attitudes toward government, 160

B.

"Baby Doe" decision, 72
Bakke, 129
Boca Raton, Florida, 102f.
Brown v. Board of Education, 31, 114, 115, 119, 121, 124, 130
Busing, school, 127, 128

C.

Carey v. Population Services International, 15, 16
Carter, President Jimmy, 138
Child care facilities, 49f.
Choice of court test, 5
Christian faith, doctrines of, 79f.
Citizenship, 97
  preferences of, 141f.
Civil rights movement, 121
Classification based on wealth, 112
Classification, suspect, 112
Cohabitation, acceptability of, 26f.
  and contraception, 14f.
  and contract law, 18
  changing attitudes toward, 19
  societal conditions affecting, 26
Colorado supreme court, 103
Commerce Clause, 93, 94, 95, 96, 97, 98, 99, 100, 106, 116, 134, 162, 167
Constitutional adjudication, 3, 17
Constitutional law and developing social forces, 52
Constitutional philosophy, 13, 110, 140f., 143, *in passim*.
Constitutional protection, 70
Contraception, 15, 16, 17
Court actions as sociological variables, 177
Court challenges, 5
Court decisions, *in passim*.
Court decisions: adults, 73ff.
  and social uncertainty, 82
  and society, 2
  children, 71f.
Court opinions, 2

D.

Death and dying issue, 68
Demetropolitanization, 89
Desegregation, attitudes toward, 121
Desegregation of schools, 116
De-urbanization and public policy, 91
Discrimination against aliens, 140, 143f.
  against pregnant women, 27
Due Process Clause, 97
Due Process Guarantee, 4
Dunn v. Blumstein, 137
Dwelling units, ceiling on, 102

E.

Edwards v. California, 92, 93, 94, 96, 100
Egalitarianism, 13
Equal protection clause, 114, 167
Ethnicity, 143
Euthanasia, 69f., 79, *in passim*.
Extramarital sexuality, tolerance for, 26f.

F.

Fair Labor Standards Act, 162, 163
Family life, value of, 23
Federal appellate court decisions and public support, 52
Federalism, issue of, 159f.
Fees, litigation involving, 136
Female employment ideology, 51
Fertility, chapter II.
Fifth Amendment, 4, 97, 104, 107
Florida District Court of Appeals, 102f.
Fourteenth Amendment, 4, 29, 93, 96, 97, 104, 107, 167
"Freedom of choice" programs, 125

Freedom of movement, 94
  intrastate, 95f.
Freedom of religious exercise, 74

G.

Garcia v. San Antonio Metropolitan Transit Authority, 162, 165f., 167
Gender, 28, 167
Gender discrimination, 98
Gender and mortality tables, 168
GI Bill, 116
Government preferences for residents, 131ff.
Guarantee of equal protection, 4, 93

H.

Harris v. McRae, 43
Hills v. Gautreaux, 112, 114
Homosexuality, attitudes of college-educated, 175
  legalized, attitude surveys, 174
Homosexual marriage, 173-176
Housing, 108
  single family preferred, 106

I.

Illegitimacy, 47ff.
Immigration attitudes, 142
Indiana supreme court, 71f.
Individual autonomy, 17f.
Institutionalization and values, 143
Invidious purpose, 112
Involvement of others in abortion, 38f.

J.

Judaism, 80
Judicial intervention constraints, 50f.

K.

Kubler-Ross, Elizabeth, 67

Laetrile, 81
Law and macro-sociological research, 177
   and social change, 176
Legal and population phenomena, interrelations between, 1
Legal development and their societal context, 81f.
Liberty, guarantee of personal, 24, 31, 140
Life-threatening conditions and adults, 73f.
Local government and population composition, 110f.
Local governmental control of population size, 100f.

M.

Malapportionment, state legislatures, 161f.
Marital stability, 41
Marriage, 21ff.
   access to, 24, 25
   and childbearing, 40
   and family life, ideals of, 23
   court recognition of importance of, 23f.
     public attitudes toward, 22
     research on, 23
     societal effects on, 26
Marvin v. Marvin, 18, 19, 20
Maryland supreme court, 107
Maryland v. Wirtz, 162, 167
Medical treatment, 79, 81
Meretricious relationships, 18
Migration and population distribution, chapter V.
Migration, freedom of, 133
   interstate, 92f., 97
   of Blacks, 115
   trend in 1970s, 90

Minors and abortion, 41f.
Minors, protection for, 25
Mississippi University for Women v. Hogan, 11, 12
Missouri, 116
Mobility, geographic, and public policy, 91
Mortality, chapter III.

N.

National Abortion Rights Action League, 36
National League of Cities v. Usery, 162, 165, 167
National Right to Life Committee, 36
New Jersey supreme court, 75, 106
New York supreme court, 103, 106

O.

Oklahoma, 116
Old Testament, 80

P.

Parental rights, 73
Pennsylvania supreme court, 104, 105, 106
Philadelphia, 105, 113
Police power, 103, 106, 107
Population control, 104
Population density, 14, *in passim*
   and attitudes, 26f.
Population growth, 101
Post-World War II ideology, 119
Predicting legal action, value of, 5f.
Pregnancy, 27-29f.
   and housing density, 30
   as legal issue, 30
Premarital sex, changing attitudes toward, 19

Privacy, right of, 16, 17, 24, 25, 26, 28f., 31, 32, 74, 176
Privileges and Immunities Clause, 96, 97, 134, 135
"Proper" jobs by gender, 13
Protestant tradition, American, 80
Purpose, governmental, 111

Q.

Quality of life, 82, 107
Quinlan, Karen, 75
"Quinlan Question," 75

R.

Racial segregation in housing, 113f.
Racial segregation, issue of, 115
"Rallying around the flag" effect, 35
Religious beliefs and affiliation, 76f.
Residence requirements for public office, 138
Residency, 134
Retirement, mandatory, 164
"Reverse discrimination," 129
Right of landowners, 103
"Right-to-Die," 70f., 73f., 82
Roe v. Wade, 31, 33, 35, 36, 38, 42, 46, 47, 130
Roman Catholic Church, 78, 79
  and abortion, 36

S.

School desegregation, 114ff.
School integration, attitudes, 121f., 124
  Supreme Court cases on, 124f.
"Separate but equal" doctrine, 114f.
Sex discrimination, 28, *in passim*
Sex roles, 9, 10, 11, 13, 30

Sex segregation in schools, 9, 10f.
Shapiro v. Thompson, 131, 132, 133
Societal problems and court decisions, 32f.
Sociology, 172f.
South, 121
  migration to, 90
State functions and federal authority, 162f.
State intervention, 72
State legislatures and political representation, 161ff.
State preferences for U.S. citizens, 139f.
State vs. federal authority, chapter V.
Sunbelt, migration to, 90f.
Supreme Court decisions and social adjustment to, 130
"Symbolic racism," 127

T.

Tax on out-migration, 92
Technological advances and death, 68
Tenth Amendment, 163, 165
Tests of constitutionality, 4
Texas, 93, 116, 143f.
Tiburon, California, 104
Travel Act, 97
"Trial marriage," public attitudes toward, 19
Truman, President Harry, 115
Tuition, charges for, 136
Twenty-Sixth Amendment, 47

U.

Urbanization, 173f.
U.S. Court of Appeals, Eighth Circuit, 136
  Eleventh Circuit, 39
  Fifth Circuit, 95
  Ninth Circuit, 50, 108, 113

Third Circuit, 10, 107
U.S. Food and Drug Administration, 81

V.

Village of Arlington Heights v. Metropolitan Housing Development Corporation. 111, 113f.
Vorchheimer v. School District of Philadelphia, 10, 11, 12

W.

Welfare assistance, 132

Welfare recipients, 131f.
West, migration to, 90
Withholding medical treatment, 71f.
Women's status, 99

Y.

Young adults, proportion in U.S. population, 46f.

Z.

Zablocki v. Redhail, 23f., 25
Zoning, 105, 106, 110, 111

ABOUT THE AUTHORS

Larry D. Barnett, associate professor of law at Widener University, holds a Ph.D. in demography from Florida State University and a J.D. from the University of Florida. He is the founder and editor of the journal, *Population Research and Policy Review*, and author of *Population Policy and the U.S. Constitution*.

Emily F. Reed, Ph. D. in political science from the University of Massachusetts, is on the staff of the Criminal Justice Council of the State of Delaware.